Rebuilding your life after redundancy

The New Life Network Handbook

2009 Edition

The **essential** one-stop shop for anyone needing to create a new and more enjoyable life after experiencing the trauma of redundancy.

Janet Davies

Published 2009 by arima publishing

www.arimapublishing.com

ISBN 978 1 84549 372 1

Printed and bound in the United Kingdom

Typeset in Palatino Linotype 11 & Arial 14/16

arima publishing
ASK House, Northgate Avenue
Bury St Edmunds, Suffolk IP32 6BB
t: (+44) 01284 700321
www.arimapublishing.com

'Most of the important things in the world have been accomplished by people who have kept on trying when there seemed to be no hope at all.'

Dale Carnegie

About the author

After graduating in marketing and finance from the University of Huddersfield, Janet Davies has held senior management positions with some of the world's top companies including American Express, Credit Suisse, NatWest, Ogilvy One and PricewaterhouseCoopers.

Today, as a Director of Davies Development Services Ltd, she has a varied portfolio of interests. She works with a variety of organisations leading talent management and business performance improvement consulting programmes, as well as being a popular public speaker, media spokesperson, writer and editor. She is also the founder and editor of the career management website www.newlifenetwork.co.uk.

A long-standing member of both the Chartered Institute of Management and the Chartered Institute of Personnel and Development, she is also a Freeman of the City of London and the Worshipful Company of Marketors.

Janet lives in Suffolk with her partner and her daughter.

For the

Aftershock Generation

Contents

Introduction

'I still believe in Hope – mostly because there's no such place as "Fingers Crossed", Arkansas.' *Molly Ivins*

The New Life Network

People ask me all the time what made me set up the New Life Network career management website (www.newlifenetwork.co.uk) and write this handbook to help people rebuild their lives after redundancy.

Well, it's pretty simple really – because it needed to be done. I had read Andrew Taylor's excellent column 'Aftershock' in *The Sunday Times* about his redundancy experience in 2005, and having gone through the trauma of it myself, I thought I might be able to help. Even in today's economic climate, redundancy can still carry a kind of 'leper status', and most of the existing information resources seem to be geared more towards *making* people redundant, rather than helping those who have been *made* redundant.

At the outset, however, contrary to all the textbooks on starting a new venture I had no specific plan, no idea how I could fund it or whether or not people would buy into the idea in significant numbers – a bit naughty really when I consider all the years I've spent working in marketing. I just had my gut instincts, enough curiosity, determination and the desire to do it and that's pretty much it. There's a lesson in there somewhere, I'm sure!

Subsequently, my research into the official facts and figures surrounding the topic showed that at least 2000 people in

England and Wales were being made redundant every working day due to some restructuring or outsourcing programme or plain old business failure – it just wasn't hitting the headlines. The Chartered Institute of Personnel and Development (CIPD) report *A barometer of HR trends and prospects 2009* indicates that 26% of their respondents have a contingency plan in place to make more redundancies over the next year. Of that 26%, 59% plan to make redundancies in the next three months. Times are going to get much tougher for everyone. So, even in 2005, there seemed to be a large enough audience for something like the support site I had in mind. Once I got started, however, I received letters and messages from visitors to the site who weren't actually being made redundant but who did have concerns over their job security or future career direction and so the content developed further to accommodate a much wider audience than I had anticipated. Research by recruiters Fish4Jobs showed that as many as four out of 10 workers are concerned about job security and there are also large numbers of so-called 'economically inactive' people (those who might want to work, if only part-time, but who don't show up on official figures because they can't or don't claim unemployment benefits, e.g. mothers on maternity leave, or those having taken early retirement) so there seemed to be a rather large number of people who could do with some sensible help and advice.

This handbook is intended to address the concerns of those people experiencing redundancy, returning to work after a career break and those who have been there, done that and want to reinvent themselves – in other words **build a new life**. It isn't meant to be some kind of long-winded, dull encyclopaedia and I have no desire to reinvent the wheel; nor is it for people who want to retire. If someone else has a fantastic website or has written (in my opinion) the definitive book on the topic, I'll say so. We have almost too much information at our disposal these days so what I'm really offering here is some practical advice and sensible short cuts based on experience and more importantly, a bit of old-fashioned good will. If you are suddenly without a job and an income, having lots of time on your hands isn't necessarily the luxury it might appear to be, so I hope that this resource will help people to get back on their feet more quickly than if they hadn't had access to it at all.

Redundancy – an old story

There's nothing new about change, redundancy and evolution; it's an old, old story. The dinosaurs disappeared, Rome fell, companies come and go, jobs have their purpose and then evolve into something else, career stars wax and wane, personal goals and circumstances move on. In 1929 the top American companies were US Steel, Standard Oil (NJ) and General Motors and the mighty Microsoft wasn't even a twinkle in anyone's eye. Who on earth would have thought of calling a company Google and that it would be worth millions of dollars? A few big brands such as Coca Cola and Levi Strauss have survived a hundred years or more but that is pretty rare.

There are many reasons why it is important that we learn to reinvent ourselves and develop new attitudes and strategies to flexible or serial careers. We now have greater expectations than ever of what we want from life for ourselves and for our families. We're living longer. The government needs us to work for longer because it can't afford to pay our pensions and neither, it seems, can many companies. Because of our declining birth rate there are fewer young people coming into the workforce than we need for our economic prosperity. Being made redundant from a job or a company is a stressful experience for most people – mortgages still need to be paid, families cared for, pension funds fed but most importantly our *talents* still need to be put to work for the benefit of our own self-esteem, society at large and the economy.

A case in point

My own career has not been without its challenges, high points and low points though I have been lucky enough to work with some incredible people and for some great companies. I graduated in 1982 and, with a recession that was biting hard, I could have wallpapered my bed-sit with the number of the 'no room at the inn'-style rejection letters I received in return. Nevertheless, I managed to find a job in finance that kept me out of trouble for a couple of years and then two years in HR which gave me skills I can honestly say have stood me in good stead ever since. The first time I came across a redundancy situation, I was a mere 26 years old. The MD and his HR aides turned up to the branch office I worked from at 9am, and by 9.05am a group of managers were marched out like the proverbial lambs to the slaughter to be advised of their fate. I was told to work from another branch but also to 'carry on as normal'. And I did.

As it happened, moving branches was a good thing because it led to career opportunities that provided me with fantastic experiences and enduring friendships with people all over the world, and enough money to fuel my shoe habit! I witnessed many more redundancies over the subsequent years. I even had to carry out a few myself, unfortunately, but I never really thought that it could happen to me. I was convinced that my diligence, my skills, my ability to build productive relationships at work, make money and reduce costs for my employers would always give me immunity from it.

And it did for many years, and then I was made redundant three times within the space of two years due to two restructures and a business downturn affecting my employers. The first time was just about bearable. I had done a good job on a big change programme I had led for four years and this had been acknowledged with top appraisal ratings and bonuses: it wasn't just my imagination or a case of egotistic self-delusion. I had delivered such reliable new tools and working practices to the organisation that I had virtually made myself redundant. I could have stayed but it would have meant relocating overseas, which just wasn't possible. Anyway, they gave me a good severance package and I went straight into another interesting job with a consulting practice. That was all going well for about a year and then the 9/11 effect had a huge impact on the revenue streams of the clients and the company I worked for, which couldn't handle the impact without casualties. We were asked to become self-employed 'associates' instead of employees to help them ride the storm, and shortly afterwards I was headhunted again for another top job. I believed that all was still well with the world as I knew it. It was sad to leave friends and colleagues behind, but grateful to be moving forward again.

The banking business of my new employer, however, was crumbling before I had even started. The work I had been asked to come in and do was nowhere near as much as I had been led to believe, and within a week I could see that the signs were not looking good. My boss told me that he had had as many as three bosses in 18 months. It was clear that he was unsupported and unconnected within the hierarchy. I could sense that the scapegoat's axe was not far away for him and that he would take a few others down with him. And so it came, but his successor was mortified that the company had not been able to live up to their promises to me and so they gave me a reasonable severance package and a good reference for the valuable work that I had nevertheless completed.

I was pretty disappointed and annoyed by this time but I didn't think it would be a problem to find another job. I had very good commercial skills, an excellent reputation for quality delivery, and so on. How wrong I was. This time it was different. The markets were bad; there were scarcely any appropriate openings around for someone of my seniority and experience, and Headhunter friends of mine were growing highly frustrated at the 'stop-go' recruiting culture prevalent with the big players who would normally be my target employers. Time was slipping steadily by, though, and I needed to keep myself busy and solvent. I was, after all, trying to provide not only for myself but also for my young daughter. I thought about what I had to offer but realised I needed to perhaps find a different way of using my skills. So, I started some part-time lecturing in marketing and management skills, which was great fun. I have always enjoyed sharing my knowledge and encouraging others to be successful and my students (department managers or MDs actually running their own businesses) appreciated having someone to guide them who had actually really done things as opposed to simply reading about them. I got to work locally sometimes for the first time in years; I had more time for my friends and family and for myself. I started to get a taste for something I hadn't had for a very, very long time – freedom! I didn't have the big salary (thank goodness for the severance cheques though!) and a Gold Class British Airways Executive Club card any more, but I also didn't have pointless meetings, endless commuting, a mountain of paperwork, permanent exhaustion and weekends spent frantically running errands that sane people do during the week. And so it was that I started to rebuild my own life, creating a portfolio career doing the things that I have always enjoyed doing: writing, research, teaching and helping companies and the people that lead them to prosper, but on my terms this time.

Then I happened to read Andrew's column and that's how this whole thing started. I could see that there was a need for someone to put together a sensible toolkit for the aftershock generation. I decided to put together my treasure chest of knowledge, experiences and that of others I knew, for the benefit of the next batch of people who will face the challenges that the myth of a job for life brings with it, and maybe those who would build a new life if only they had the courage, the good sense, the time or frankly the encouragement to do so. Who knew, even then, that the current credit crisis and recession would create even more need for this book and the resources on the New Life website?

The New Life Network, then, will endeavour to provide a helpful and inspiring resource for all of those who know that redundant doesn't mean 'finished', that 'over 40' doesn't mean 'over the hill', that 'unemployed' doesn't mean 'unemployable', and that careers and skills must be flexible and move with the times. It's for those who know that new and fulfilling lives can and must be built to replace the old ones we had, whatever our age, background or circumstances.

Finally, I would like to thank the thousands of visitors to the site so far, for their inspiring messages and stories, help and selfless contribution of material and references for the book.

Good luck and happy hunting!

Janet Davies

Founder and editor of the New Life Network
www.newlifenetwork.co.uk
February 2009

Chapter 1 Redundancy

If you suspect that redundancy might be on the cards for you in the future, or if you are currently experiencing the process, in the first instance it pays to know the facts and understand what your rights actually are. Redundancy is stressful and it is easy to panic if you don't have a confident command of independent facts and advice.

Internally your Human Resources contact should be able to supply you with much of this information but I appreciate that this may not be timely, possible or appropriate. As they say, forewarned is forearmed. At the end of this chapter there is a table summarising key facts and procedures.

Every organisation has its own way of going about redundancy selection and communication, calculating payments, post-redundancy support and so on. There are, however, laws they have to abide by and standards of best practice they are advised to follow, not least because of the potential harm to their reputation and other risks to their organisation if they are involved in a badly implemented redundancy programme. Any firm (including the public sector) intending to make 20 or more employees redundant within a period of 90 days or less must submit form HR1 to the Department for Business Enterprise & Regulatory Reform of Trade and Industry (BERR) for monitoring and response. Thirty day's notice are required unless more than 100 redundancies are planned, in which case the notice period is 90 days.

The Office for National Statistics defines a redundancy as a situation where 'an employee leaves their job because the position no longer exists. This may be the result of a fall in an organisation's demand for labour, a re-structuring of the organisation, or a combination of both.'

There are plenty of places for employers to go to find out the facts on processes and the law regarding notice periods, redundancy payments and so on, and I will point you in their direction throughout the handbook if I think they'll help. For those being made redundant, however, the sources of pertinent information are harder to track down – this is where the New Life Network resources really come into their own!

Firstly though, let's look at the reasons for redundancy as well as its effects and how that may give us some clues as to what the writing on the walls is telling us.

What redundancy means

The concise Oxford Dictionary defines the word redundant as:

redundant *adj.* **1.** superfluous; not needed. **2.** that can be omitted without any loss of significance. **3.** *Brit.* (of a person) no longer needed at work and therefore unemployed.

I think it is the first two of the three definitions that leads to the process of redundancy being so personally painful for many people. It's not just the fear that accompanies the actual redundancy process; it's the threat to one's financial security, self-esteem and future survival. Even when we know that there was nothing we could have done about it and that our selection for redundancy wasn't really personal, it can still hurt. It makes people feel vulnerable and touchy when they look for work afterwards and it is often the emotional baggage that person carries with them that gets in the way of finding a new life more quickly and easily.

Then there is the further complication of age and attitude. Let's face it, there are some people out there who by their own intransigence, complacency or lack of competence have put not only their own jobs but also those of others in jeopardy. If these people have come from the older ranks of a workforce, it is easy for mature workers to be labelled as inflexible and unable to move with changing times. Then that label sticks to all mature workers whether it's true or not and that's how stereotypes are born. The employers want to minimise their risk when they hire new people. They tell the recruiters they want 'energetic, self-motivated, results-oriented' candidates, a subtle subtext for 'no one over 40', and sure enough the age barrier (so easy to apply) becomes a cut-off point that leaves many talented and experienced people high and dry.

The new legislation on **age discrimination** which came into effect in 2006 was meant to put a stop to all that and the demographic time bomb we have in the UK (which means we have more people retiring than we have young people to work and pay taxes to keep them in hip replacements and Werthers Originals) is scarily close to detonation. In Europe in 1940, 48% of the workforce was under 30, whereas that number had dropped to 22% by the year 2000. By 2030 it is estimated that 34% of the working population will be over 50 and less than 20% under 30.

So, will the new laws change anything? Yes, of course they will (not least because of the sheer shortage of labour in the future) but probably slowly, and without the real economic and attitudinal impact that we need right now. The Equal Opportunities Act brought an end to much obvious and ridiculous discrimination against women in the workplace. Thirty years ago 15.4 million men were in work and only 9.4 million women. Now, there are still 15.4 million men in work but the number of women in work has shot up to 13.2 million. The latest research by Cranfield University, however, still shows that women have not gained access to the corridors of power in significant numbers. In fact, they found that the number of FTSE 100 companies with women directors has fallen for the third year running. Baroness Sarah Hogg, the Chair of 3i, the venture capital group, is the only British female head of a FTSE 100 company. Only 17 of the top 20 FTSE companies are women. Cases of sexual harassment and discrimination still hit the headlines every week. Gaps in take-home pay between men and women are also still quite large despite the Equal Pay Act (1970). Women who work full-time, for example, earn 18% less than men and women part-timers earn 40% less. Women do appear, however, to rule the top jobs in education and the media. According to Simon Howard, reporting for The Times, women also choose accountancy more than any other profession, though law and medicine are increasing in popularity. Some of this is, of course, partly the result of numerous campaigns to change attitudes to women in the professions, but this is mainly due to a consistent decline in male performance in the education system. There are now fewer suitably qualified men available to join the professions. In 2004 only 41% of the 2:1 or 1st class degrees required by the major law and accountancy firms were gained by men who were in the minority among students.

So new lifers, men and women alike, will have to find creative ways to play the age discrimination game and still win. Paying attention to your appearance; avoiding body language that transmits cynicism and apathy; keeping up with the trends and information that affect your area of work, and then being able to project that enthusiastically in an interview are all extra little tricks that can help in the battle against being consigned to the scrap heap. Hopefully, everyone will find helpful inspiration or at least a tip or two in this handbook.

Reasons for redundancy

There are essentially five key reasons for redundancies within companies.

1. **Reduction in business income** leading to a requirement to reduce their costs accordingly. This may be due to various **external** forces named by management guru Igor Ansoff as P.E.S.T.L.E – political, economic, social, technological, legal or environmental forces. So, a new law may make trading conditions difficult or interest rates (and the current credit crisis) may make borrowing or buying more expensive or difficult. The internet has totally revolutionised the way we do business that few originally predicted. It has made some jobs or companies obsolete (and thank goodness, because some of them were truly awful) but created a whole swathe of new ones. Or it could be due to **internal** forces, i.e. the business not being managed properly, ineffective marketing, poor quality products, not anticipating a market opportunity or reacting to a threat, e.g. a competitor, delivering poor customer service or value for money. So, some trading difficulties are hard to avoid because they are not within the control of the company (although many employ powerful lobbies to minimise their risk pertaining to laws or regulations that may affect them when implemented); and some could be avoided because the organisation could have invested in higher calibre people, training, products or tools or have made better decisions to promote prosperity and survival.

2. **Efficiency reasons** Because of a mix of both external and internal forces, jobs (and therefore people) may become redundant. A technological breakthrough, a lowering of cost to acquire that technology and a savvy

management that implements a new process or creates a new market, can mean that some jobs disappear – but invariably new ones emerge, even if they are outside the company you may already work for. Sometimes our skills are transferable in ways that we couldn't have imagined and sometimes we have to retrain and learn to do something else for which there is a demand.

3. **A new broom** A new leader may well have been brought in on a modernising or financial agenda and will go through an organisation like a dose of salts questioning (or at least employing large packs of consultants to question) every action, every person, every transaction and every practice, with a view to taking out jobs that may be unnecessary, unproductive, anachronistic or just plain unpopular. In such cases, my advice is usually this: when a new sheriff rides into town you have three choices – you can either help them to lead, follow them constructively or get out of their way. Some people, however, choose another route that I call the 'Eric Clapton' method – they shoot the sheriff. This is a strategy that usually results in many casualties, often quite unnecessarily, but the blood is spilt anyway. Does that ring any bells?

4. **Hostile take-over or merger** Usually when a company is taken over there will be opportunities to maximise profitability by centralising or merging key processes, particularly administrative functions. Key staff (of whatever rank) may be retained for a while on the understanding that they will be looked after (i.e. paid more than the statutory minimum redundancy package plus other perks) when the time comes for them to move on. Many see the writing on the wall for life as they have previously known it, and start creating an exit plan to jump before they are pushed. I know plenty of people who have timed this beautifully, have lined up another, better job *and* pocketed a nice little lump sum. I know

lots of others who haven't, who hung on for dear life and when the axe came were totally unprepared for the effects. If your company takes over or is taken over by another company you should **expect** change.

5. **Outsourcing** (or 'outsorcery' as some of my more cynical friends call it). These days, lots of companies transfer whole legions of jobs or functions to China, India or some other place. It's not that important where they go, really, it just means that it's not where you used to have a job. Some of these programmes are well thought-out and the cost reductions do make a difference that protects other jobs in the long run. Many, unfortunately, are not. Everyone has a story about having to talk to someone who doesn't understand what you want or what you are saying or keeps you on hold listening to appalling music after you've gone through 20 different options, only to then cut you off after 20 minutes of hell. Unfortunately, many poorly run operations are just transferred to someone else who also does a poor job. The fact is if your job in a call centre, IT department or HR function is gone, you simply have to find another one.

There are other less common reasons for redundancy, such as the death of an employer in a small firm, illegal practices leading to enforced closure, and so on, but the five above account for the most common causes. The Chartered Institute of Personnel and Development (CIPD) report *A barometer of HR trends and prospects 2009* indicates that the main reasons for making redundancies are restructuring (70%) and to reduce costs (60%). Managers and professionals have been the most affected (38%), followed by skilled non-manual workers (23%).

Redundancy packages

Depending on the reason for the redundancy, the size and profile of the company, their standing in the community and so on, there will be greater or smaller amounts of latitude relative to the redundancy packages on offer. The table on redundancy basics at the end of the chapter shows what the boundaries of the law are but many companies will offer better financial packages, extensions on healthcare benefits, deals on bonuses, outplacement help and retraining than they are legally obliged to. The 2009 CIPD report also indicates that two in five organisations (40%) do not offer redundancy pay above the statutory minimum. A third (35%) always offer this, with a further 14% offering it depending on seniority or length of service.

Sometimes you might be asked to sign something called a **'confidentiality'** or **'compromise' agreement**. These are usually reserved for executive or managerial level staff but it's worth knowing what they are.

A 'compromise agreement' is a legally binding agreement following the termination of your employment in certain circumstances. It usually provides for a severance payment from your employer, in return for which you agree not to pursue any claim you may have to an employment tribunal. Quite often, the compromise agreement will also deal with the notice element in your contract of employment and may provide for a payment in lieu.

The unkind among us might think this is just another expression for 'hush money' but if you were going to have to leave anyway, and signing one of these agreements means you get more money, depending on how compromised the parties might be, it's got to be worth considering. However, you shouldn't be asked to sign one without the advice of a solicitor and the firm has to pay all reasonable costs of that.

It's funny how, when the signs of redundancy start – closed doors, lots of emergency meetings called off-site, mutterings and rumour-mongering, an excessive number of visits by consultants or senior ranking employees from HQ – contracts of employment that haven't seen the light of day suddenly become more well studied than a pools coupon. You may have had concerns about your contract before you started your job or while you were doing it, but at this point you will certainly want to know what happens if you leave, voluntarily or otherwise. For example, if you are made redundant, there may be issues relating to notice, outstanding bonus entitlement and the enforceability of restrictive covenants (whom you may or may not be able to work with in the future, concerns relative to poaching clients, etc.). There may also be issues about whether final salary payments, such as payment in lieu of notice, can be made free of tax, and concerns about pensions and share schemes. Again, this depends on how your employment contract is drafted. There are lots of places you can go to for specific help if you have serious concerns, from specialist law firms to Citizen's Advice Bureaux.

Once the process of consultation has been completed, you should know exactly what's happening in terms of your pay and so on. Even though you might be feeling wretched, it's worth keeping a clear head to ensure you have the following items of key paperwork sorted before you leave. You will need the first two in order to claim any benefits you might be entitled to.

- **P45 form** You need this to give to your next employer or to claim benefit, so make sure you know when your ex-employer will have it available and how you will get it.

- **Redundancy payment details** These must be in writing, outlining amounts, dates, etc.
- **Company support arrangements** Names, telephone numbers and addresses of outplacement contacts or financial advisors retained to help you.
- A copy of any **references** your employer will provide for you, CVs, copies of appraisals, etc., to help you with your future job search.
- If you **change your address** after leaving the company, don't forget to let the company know so that they can send you any paperwork and communicate with you. You should also (just in case of any queries) take a basic contact sheet with you (phone, fax, emails) for people such as your:

  - line manager(s)
  - HR staff
  - union or staff representative
  - pension fund trustees
  - private medical insurance supplier
  - company doctor.

Managing your emotions

The driving force for the redundancy will often have an impact on the fall out that individuals feel. These are all quite natural reactions and they are examined more closely in Chapter 3, on coping with stress.

- **Anger and resentment** can build because a person may feel that they had seen disaster coming, had done their best to try to prevent it and because they weren't listened to, jobs were forfeited (especially if one of them happened to be theirs). It's natural to feel angry and you need to work through this rather than suppress it, to pass to a more positive frame of mind.

- *Schadenfreude* (the German term for enjoying someone else's misfortune while muttering 'I told you so'). It can be a source of comfort when, long after you have left, the management backlash occurs and everyone finds out that their 'outsorcery' decision (or whatever other misguided management fad or appointment was ineptly dealt with) was an utter disaster. But *Schadenfreude* mostly just stores up cynicism and is best discarded.

- **Bitterness** can occur if an individual believes that they were picked for redundancy because of their age, race, gender or some other illegal practice that just can't be proved. If you can't prove it and you can't obtain justice through the tribunal system, it's probably best just to let go and get on with your life. If you can prove it, it could well be helpful to others, not just yourself, to pursue the matter through the proper channels to put paid to an iniquitous practice.

- **Thoughts of revenge and getting even** These can often arise as a result of a combination of issues but especially where an individual feels stitched up, or betrayed (especially if others keep *their* job), or unfairly selected because of some personal reason or to settle an old score. It can be very beneficial to allow those feelings to emerge so that you can get rid of them – because it's likely that any plots you hatch could hurt you the most. By all means vent your spleen and have a good rant to the hamster, the dog or any inanimate object of your choosing: just get it off your chest. Then get on with building your new life – the one that is going to be much better than the old one.

- **Depression, sadness and general unhappiness or lassitude** If you've put your life and soul into something it's only natural to mourn its loss and perhaps fear that nothing else can take its place. Going through those emotions and staying in touch with old colleagues can help a lot in these situations and speed up the healing process.

• **Napoleon Hill**, protégé of American industrialist and philanthropist Andrew Carnegie and author of the best-selling book *Think and Grow Rich*, identifies the seven major negative feelings as fear, jealousy, hatred, revenge, greed, superstition and anger; and the six basic fears as poverty, criticism, ill health, lost love, old age and death. His book is an excellent read (not soppy or new-agey) and I recommend it to anyone who is experiencing any of these fears and emotions to help find a way to work through them on the road to building that new life you're going to be needing.

Redundancy facts at a glance

Disclaimer
Things change constantly and everyone's circumstances can be different so while I endeavour to give you the facts as they stand today, it is essential that you visit http://www.berr.gov.uk/whatwedo/employment/employment-legislation/employment-guidance/page15686.html to get the exact and current information as it pertains to you and your situation.

What redundancy means	Redundancy is a form of dismissal caused by your employer's need to reduce his or her workforce. Redundancy may happen because a work place is closing down, or because fewer employees are (or are expected to be) needed for work of a particular kind. Normally your job must have disappeared for redundancy to be justified.

What redundancy means	It is not redundancy if your employer immediately takes on a direct replacement for you. The employer then lays him or herself open to claims of unfair dismissal. It will not matter, however, if your employer is recruiting more people for work of a different kind, or in another location (unless you were required by contract to move to the new location).
Making redundancies	An employer proposing collective redundancies is required to consult in advance with representatives of the affected employees, and to notify the projected redundancies to the DTI. A collective redundancy situation arises where **20 or more** employees are to be made redundant at one establishment within a period of **90** days or less. Consultation must be completed before any notices of dismissal are issued to employees. A complaint of failure to consult may be made to an employment tribunal, and must normally be brought within three months of the last of the dismissals. Where a complaint is upheld, the tribunal may make a protective award to employees of up to 90 days' pay. In addition, the government is considering the case for making a small legislative change to make clear that notifications to the DTI must be made before any redundancy notices are sent to affected employees.

	Sometimes employers try to dodge the legal requirements by making redundancies in blocks smaller than 20 across intervals of more than 90 days.
Unfair selection for redundancy	Dismissal on grounds of redundancy will be unfair if the employee was selected for redundancy when others in similar circumstances were not selected, and the reason for this was: • the employee's trade union membership or activities or non-membership of a trade union* • that the employee had sought, in good faith, to exercise a statutory employment protection right • that the employee took, or proposed to take, certain specified types of action on health and safety grounds • on maternity-related grounds • for taking or seeking to take paternity leave • for taking or seeking to take adoption leave • for requesting flexible working arrangements

	<ul><li>the employee was a shop worker or a betting worker and was selected for redundancy for refusing or proposing to refuse to do shop work or betting work on Sundays; or he was selected for redundancy for giving, or proposing to give, an 'opting-out' notice to his employer</li><li>for performing, or proposing to perform, any duties relevant to his or her role as an employee occupational pension scheme trustee</li><li>for performing, or proposing to perform, any duties relevant to his or her role as an employee representative or as a candidate to be a representative of this kind</li><li>for reasons relating to the national minimum wage</li><li>for reasons relating to the Working Time Regulations 1998</li><li>for making a protected disclosure within the meaning of the Public Interest Disclosure Act 1998</li><li>because he or she took or sought to take parental leave, time off for dependants, ordinary maternity leave or additional maternity leave</li></ul>

	<ul><li>where action started on or after 24 April 2000, because they took lawfully organised official industrial action lasting eight weeks or less (or more than eight weeks, in certain circumstances)</li><li>for exercising or seeking to exercise rights relating to trade union recognition procedures</li><li>for performing or proposing to perform any duties relating to an employee's role as a workforce representative or as a candidate to be such a representative for the purposes of the Trans-national Information and Consultation of Employees Regulations 1999, or for taking certain actions in connection with these regulations, or for proposing to take or failing to take such actions</li><li>for reasons relating to the Part-time Workers (Prevention of Less Favourable Treatment) Regulations 2000</li><li>for reasons relating to the Tax Credits Act 2002</li><li>for reasons relating to the Fixed-term Employees (Prevention of Less Favourable Treatment) Regulations 2002</li></ul>

- for reasons relating to the European Public Limited-Liability Company Regulations 2004

- from 6 April 2005, for reasons relating to the Information and Consultation of Employees Regulations 2004 for undertakings with 150 employees (from 6 April 2007 for undertakings with 100 employees and from 6 April 2008 for undertakings with 50 employees)

- from 6 April 2005, for reasons relating to jury service

Furthermore, dismissal on the grounds of redundancy may also be held to be unfair (depending upon the circumstances) for some other reason (for example, if the employer failed to give adequate warning of redundancy or failed to consider alternative employment for the employee).

*Dismissal relating to trade union membership or activities or non-membership of a union

A dismissal will be held to be unfair if the main reason for it was either that the employee was, or proposed to become, a

	member of an independent trade union; or had taken part, or proposed to take part, in the activities of an independent trade union, if the activities were outside working hours or in accordance with an arrangement with the employer permitting the employee to take part in such activities during working hours; or that the employee was not a member of a trade union, or had refused or proposed to refuse to become or remain a member. *There is no qualifying period of service, or upper age limit for employees who wish to complain that they have been dismissed for either of these reasons.*
When is a redundancy payment due?	Your employer must give you a lump-sum payment if you: • are made redundant • have at least two years' continuous service since the age of 18 (service before the age if 18 does not count for these purposes) • meet the other conditions set out in this table. You may also be entitled to other non-statutory payments if this has been agreed in your contract of employment.

Who can qualify?	You will receive payment only if you are an employee working under a contract of employment. Self-employed people and members of a partnership do not qualify under the Act though they may have separate contractual agreements.
	Directors and other office holders may be employees if they work under a contract of employment. They will not qualify if they do not work under a contract of employment.
	Contracts of employment may be spoken or written and last for any length of time or be fixed. In law, employees generally have a contract as soon as they start work and by doing so prove that they accept the conditions offered by the employer.
Who may not be entitled to a redundancy payment?	The following categories of employees have no right to a redundancy payment under the Act: • employees whose service ends on or after their 65th birthday • employees who work in a job with a normal retirement age of less than 65 and who have reached that age • members of the Armed Forces • House of Lords and House of Commons staff • apprentices whose service ends at the end of the apprenticeship

	contract • employees at the end of a fixed-term contract which was agreed, renewed or extended before October 1st 2002 and lasts at least two years, where they have already given written agreement to waive their entitlement to a redundancy payment at the end of the contract. Any waivers inserted into contracts agreed, renewed or extended after October 1st 2002 will not be valid and fixed-term employees will have a right to statutory redundancy payments if they have been continuously employed for two years or more and are made redundant • domestic servants working in a private home who are members of the employer's immediate close family • share fishermen paid only by a share in the proceeds of the catch • Crown servants or employees in a public office • employees of the government of an overseas territory
What are the payments?	The amount of your lump-sum redundancy payment depends on: • how long you have been continuously employed by your

	employer; • how your years of continuous service relate to a particular age band ; • your weekly pay, up to a legal limit. • For each complete year of continuous service between the ages of 18 and 21, you will receive half a week's pay; • for each complete year of continuous service between the ages of 22 and 40, you will receive one week's pay; • for each complete year of continuous service between the ages of 41 and 65 you will receive 1 week's pay. However, if you are over 64, the total amount of the payment you receive will be reduced. If you are aged between 64 and 65, the amount due will be reduced by one-twelfth for every complete month you are over 64. • To help you work out your payment, you can use the ready reckoners you will find on the DTI website (www.dti.gov.uk) for calculating the number of week's pay due. • For various reasons some companies will pay above these statutory minimums but they are not obliged to do so.

Will I pay tax on the payment?	You will not pay income tax on a **statutory** redundancy payment, although other redundancy payments you receive from your employer may be taxable - see the Inland Revenue booklet *Income tax and redundancy: a guide to tax and National Insurance Contributions* IR143. Normally your employer may set the payments against tax as business expense. **At time of writing, you should not have to pay tax on redundancy payments up to £30,000 as a result of Inland Revenue exemptions.**
Can I still claim Jobseeker's Allowance?	A **statutory** redundancy payment will have no effect on any entitlement you may have to **contribution-based** Jobseeker's Allowance. Savings of £8000 (which your redundancy lump sum will be considered part of) will disqualify you from claiming **income-based** Jobseeker's Allowance.
What if I think I have grounds for applying to an employment tribunal?	• If you disagree with your employer about your entitlement to a redundancy payment, you can take the matter to an employment tribunal. You can do this at any time. But you may lose your right to a payment if you do not take certain steps within six months of the day your job ends, or the date

any new job ends with your employer, an associated employer or an employer who takes over the business. If you have made a written claim to your employer or contacted an employment tribunal within six months, you cannot lose your right to a payment because of delay.

- If you do not take any of the steps mentioned above within the first six months, but take one of those steps within the following six months, the employment tribunal may still decide that you should receive a payment. They will consider the reason for the delay and all the circumstances.
- If you want to apply to a tribunal ask at a Jobcentre Plus office for a form IT1 and leaflet or phone the helpline: 0845 145 0004.
- When you apply to an employment tribunal, you should name your employer as 'respondent' on the application form. If your employer is insolvent, you should add the words 'in receivership' or 'in liquidation' to your employer's name as appropriate. You should give the name and address of the receiver or liquidator separately, if you know it.
- If the tribunal awards you a redundancy payment, but you do

	not receive it, you need to ask the Redundancy Payments Office for advice.
Voluntary redundancy	Non-compulsory selection could be by **voluntary redundancy**. This is a more expensive method for the employer since long-serving employees may be attracted to higher redundancy settlements. It is not uncommon for employers to offer higher redundancy payments as an incentive for staff to leave. However, this method may result in a disparity in the remaining experience and skills and affect the productivity of the company. Indeed, many redundancy agreements approve the employer's right to decide on who should be allowed voluntary redundancy and who should not. So if an employee applies for voluntary redundancy it is not certain that it will be allowed. The employee should also consider whether a failed application would affect future career prospects. Another method for non-compulsory selection could be by early retirement, again more expensive, but on the positive side it has less serious effects on the morale of the workforce.

Essential resources

www.newlifenetwork.co.uk
Everything you need to know about coping with redundancy, how to find a new job, set up your own business or retraining.

www.berr.gov.uk
The Department of Business Enterprise & Regulatory Reform (BERR) an excellent site and although it is more employer- than employee-biased, it pays to know what your employer should actually be doing by law.

www.acas.org.uk
ACAS is an organisation devoted to preventing and resolving employment disputes and contains lots of free information on redundancy matters.

Chapter 2 Managing your finances

Adjusting your finances

Redundancy can bring with it the fear of financial insecurity, even if that doesn't prove to be the reality. This chapter is dedicated to pointing you in the right direction when it comes to dealing with your finances, whatever your circumstances.

Understanding your current commitments

If you don't already have a document that outlines all of your **outgoings** and **income,** now is the time to set one up. You only need a simple spreadsheet, handwritten or preferably set up on a computer in Excel or another basic software application. You can download a free template at www.newlifenetwork.co.uk/managing-your-finances-c70.html.

Once you can understand exactly where your money goes every month and what income (if any) you have coming in, it will be easier to see where you can **make economies** or how long you can manage without a regular income from another job. Some items, such as insurance premiums, might be pretty much fixed and it would be difficult (although not impossible) to change them mid-year; but many will be relatively variable and more likely to be targets for savings.

The example table gives you a basic idea of how to lay your spreadsheet out. Your entries will vary according to your lifestyle, so change the headings as necessary. Setting out a monthly sheet will show you where you have lows or spikes of expenditure to plan for. You might be able to go on to budget or monthly payment plans to even out those highs and lows, and make budgeting easier.

Example spreadsheet

Outgoing	Monthly amount £	Incoming	Monthly amount £
Mortgage	600.00	Benefits	300.00
Council Tax	120.00	Interest income	100.00
Telephone	20.00		
TV licence	10.00		
Health insurance	20.00		
Water charges	30.00		
Insurance buildings	50.00		
Mobile	25.00		
Travel/car	50.00		
Car park	10.00		
Groceries	400.00		
Total	**1335.00**		**400.00**
Savings			
Bank savings	3000.00		
Investments (Premium Bonds, ISAs, etc.)	3000.00		
	6000.00		

- There may be other things worth digging out for examination, such as insurance that you own but haven't ever needed to claim on before. So, if you do have an

insurance policy to protect your mortgage payments or credit card payments, look it up, read the small print and, if you are entitled to, make a claim as soon as you can.

- If you have any assets, such as savings that you can use to tide you over a bad patch, work out how long you can make them last and ensure that the money is put somewhere with the best access and interest rates.

- If you will be receiving a **lump sum** and you have another job or income stream coming along immediately, you might want to consult an IFA (independent financial advisor) or other trusted advisor on the best way to deal with your windfall.

- If you are worried about your mortgage talk to your lender as soon as possible. They may let you take a payment holiday or switch to interest only payments to tide you over until you are back on your feet again.

- Getting a **part-time job,** even if it's not at the level you're used to, could be a good way of keeping some money coming in while still allowing you the flexibility to job hunt and attend interviews.

- However difficult it may be, it is best to **share** this information with your **family** so that everyone can help to be careful about spending priorities and aware of savings that can be made.

Managing with less – where could you save some money?

Not being at work does mean that you'll spend less on transport, buying your lunch, child care, etc., so you may find that you need a little less money than you anticipated to survive. It could also be prudent to economise in case your next job doesn't pay as well as your previous one, or if it will take time to build up overtime pay or bonus entitlements. When you are really busy at work and cash rich, time poor, it's easy to justify certain types of expenditure – ready meals, cleaners, etc. When you are cash poor, time rich you have time to re-examine your spending patterns. Once you start looking, you might be amazed at how wasteful you can be and how easy it is to cut down in certain ways.

- If you smoke, why not use this as your perfect opportunity to stop? Smoking 20 cigarettes a day at around £5 a pack costs approximately £140 a month. You'll save lots of money and safeguard your health at the same time.

- Do you buy lots of ready meals and convenience foods? You could improve your diet and your budget by cooking meals from scratch. You've got time to watch the pennies now and make proper meals. If you don't know how to cook, learning might pass the time and you'll probably enjoy your new skills.

- Do you pay for domestic help that you could cut down on or make do without until you're working again?

- Are all of your utilities (gas, electricity, water and telephone) with the most advantageous providers?

You could go on the internet and resear deals that you probably didn't have time to before.

- You could save on your gas or electric bills in other ways. Could you turn down your heating a few notches? (The National Energy Foundation recommends setting the thermostat at 20°C/68°F.) Could you turn off lights when you leave a room and turn appliances off at night? Could you use your time to fix a leaky tap, or put in some insulation that you didn't bother about before? If your water is metered, showers cost less than baths, and washing up by hand uses less water than a dishwasher.

- What about your mobile phone bill? Could you downgrade your contract, use Pay as You Go – or get rid of it altogether?

- Could you travel by bus, walk or cycle to wherever you need to go instead of using your car all the time?

- Do you have a gym membership that you pay for but hardly ever use? Now you have the time, could you use it more or otherwise cancel it and find another way to exercise instead?

- Could you find cash in your attic? Clearing the clutter could be good for your soul but you might make a few quid at a car boot sale, on eBay or through the free ads in your local paper.

- Are you borrowing on credit cards? Get rid of them if you can. Otherwise, make sure you pay them off at the end of the month to avoid high interest charges or find somewhere else to borrow the money from at a lower interest rate. Could you swap to interest-free arrangements or transfer your current balances?

- Have you got the best mortgage rate deal?

- If you have savings, are they in the most high-yield accounts?

- Shop around for the best deals when you renew insurance for your home or car.

- You don't have to be socially isolated and you don't have to spend a lot of money to have fun either. It's even more important to have some fun to keep your spirits up. Instead of going out for meals, could you invite friends around and cook for them instead? How about a few pot-luck suppers where everyone brings a course?

For more ideas about saving money Martin Lewis's excellent site www.moneysavingexpert.com is a really great resource and he offers a free newsletter with up-to-date money-saving tips.

Claiming benefit

If you have been in gainful employment all your life you probably have no idea what **benefits** you may or may not be entitled to until you find a new job, let alone how to go about applying for them. You might also feel very uncomfortable about it.

Remember that if you've been paying National Insurance contributions for years, state benefits are not handouts or charity – you've paid your way and you have a right to them. Contrary to what some of the tabloids would have us believe, however, the benefit system is not an endless road paved with gold (in 2009, the maximum Jobseeker's Allowance for someone over 25 is just £60.0 per week) and the vast majority of people would much rather be earning money and deciding what to do with it on their own terms anyway.

The uncertainty of not knowing when some real money might flow back into your household is often hard to live with, so finding out about benefits and readjusting your finances just has to be done. The sooner you find out about what you can and can't claim for, the better it will be. Claims are not normally backdated on the grounds of ignorance of the process – or on any other grounds for that matter.

NB: the rules and regulations regarding benefits change from time to time, loopholes are closed, and new initiatives are launched. So, while the basics are outlined here, *you must check your own individual circumstances with the relevant authorities.* You can go directly to the Government site on the internet at www.jobcentreplus.gov.uk to research all the current rules and regulations.

The benefits agencies make a pretty clear distinction between those who have redundancy payments, savings and investments to help them survive their period of unemployment and those who don't (if you have savings over £8000 you will not qualify for income-based Jobseeker's Allowance). You will need to complete the exercise on your expenses and income sources before you attend a benefits interview and take the appropriate documentation along with you.

If you have significant savings or a redundancy settlement you may still be able to claim contributions-based Jobseeker's Allowance, although this is subject to a time limit of 24 weeks. Once it runs out, if you still have savings that disqualify you from claiming non-contributions-based benefit, you may receive nothing unless you transfer to another programme, like New Deal, or one that, for example, might help you to set up your own business.

There are other advantages of Jobseeker's Allowance to be considered:

- your National Insurance will continue to be paid, so you should not have a contributions gap;
- you may qualify for free prescriptions, eye tests and dental care;
- you may qualify for other things, like free access to local-authority owned sports facilities, etc.

Low-income families may also receive help for any children still at school. The Educational Maintenance Allowance (EMA) is for sixth formers who can qualify for up to £30 a week if your income is below £30K a year and young people at university may qualify for student loans and paid tuition fees. You can find out more at www.dfes.gov.uk/financialhelp/ema/.

Tax credits (working or child) are also well worth applying for, again if your household income is under £30K per annum. You can check online if you are entitled at: www.hmrc.gov.uk/individuals/tmatax-credits.shtml. At time of writing online claims can no longer be accepted due to a fraud issue currently being resolved.

The claim process

Whether you are an unskilled, unemployed person or a former senior executive, the claim process is exactly the same – the old Executive and Professional Register track (for those who can remember it) doesn't exist any longer. There are employment offices (Job Centres) dotted all over the country, usually open 9 am–5 pm, Monday to Friday. Each one has a different local telephone number that can be found at www.jobcentreplus.gov.uk. Alternatively, there is a text phone number (0800 023 4888) or you can just walk in and find out the best way to get your first appointment. You will be asked to bring a series of documents to prove your eligibility and identity and to fill in quite a few forms, so a degree of patience and organisation is required. Benefit fraud is rife so it is not unlikely that you will feel you are being treated as 'guilty until proven innocent'. This is very annoying but has to be stoically endured.

There is an important clue in the title of the benefit. Jobseeker's Allowance means just that and you will need to provide regular fortnightly feedback on your efforts and the outcomes of your job seeking. Setting up a simple spreadsheet (like the one recommended earlier) and printing it off every fortnight to take with you to the employment office should help the process. Job Centre offices tend to be clean, smoke-free, comfortable and modern places and the staff generally empathetic. There will always be exceptions to this of course. It helps if you arrive at your appointments on time, have the correct information to hand and have a positive attitude to finding employment. There are plenty of people who pitch up at these places with none of these things and who appear to have left their manners at home as well, so the job can be tough for the staff as well as the claimants. Sadly, many seem to feel the need to employ security guards on the premises.

Chapter 3 Coping emotionally with redundancy and change

'If you lose hope, somehow you lose the vitality that keeps life moving, you lose that courage to be, that quality that helps you go on in spite of it all. And so today I still have a dream.'
Martin Luther King Jr

Facing the prospect of redundancy, living through the process and the aftermath can take a huge toll on us emotionally. This chapter is dedicated to advice and help on how to cope with the emotional stresses and strains that come with letting go of the old and ushering in the new.

The Life Change Unit score

The Life Change Unit (LCU) score is a measure of individual stress relating to the impact of stress on health. The research to produce this index was conducted by Dr Thomas Holmes and Dr Richard Rahe of the School of Medicine, University of Washington, USA. Over a period of twenty years the researchers were able to assign a numerical value to a range of life events and rank them in order of importance.

According to Holmes and Rahe, if an individual's LCUs total 150–199 he or she stands a mild chance of illness in the following year, with 200–299 indicating a moderate risk. Over 300 LCUs puts a person in a category where they are very likely to suffer serious physical or emotional illness. The loss of your job rates 47 LCUs on the scale. You can see the rest on the following table. The message is clear: people should try to regulate the changes in their lives, many of which will be in their control, and try to stagger their incidence and intensity. So, be aware and take care of yourself, especially where smoking, drinking and drugs are concerned.

The schedule of recent events (the Holmes-Rahe scale of Life Change Units)

Event	LCU	Event	LCU
Death of a spouse	100	Change in work responsibilities	30
Martial separation	65	Son/daughter leaving home	29
Death of a close family member	63	Trouble with in-laws	29
Personal illness or injury	53	Outstanding personal achievement	29
Marriage	50	Wife beginning or stopping work	29
Loss of job	47	Revision of personal habits	24
Marital reconciliation	45	Trouble with work superior	23
Retirement	45	Change in work hours/conditions	20
Change in health of a family member	44	Change in residence	20
Wife's pregnancy	40	Change in schools	20
Sexual difficulties	39	Change in recreation	19

Gain of a new family member	39	Change in social activities	18
Change in financial status	38	Taking out a small mortgage	17
Death of a close friend	37	Change in sleeping habits	16
Change to a different kind of work	36	Change in number of family get-togethers	15
Increase or decrease in arguments	35	Change in eating habits with spouse	15
Taking out a bigger mortgage	31	Holiday	13
Foreclosure of mortgage or loan	30	Minor violations of law	11

Some jobs are more stressful than others, so losing a stressful job may actually bring some countermeasure of relief with it. In 1987 the University of Manchester Institute of Science and Technology (UMIST) conducted some research into stressful jobs, rating them on a scale of 1 to 10. A selection of their results is to be found in the table below.

If you are coming out of or considering going in to one of these areas you may be interested in their findings. I wonder if the passage of time and the march of technology would alter their position if they were to conduct the research again?

Profession/job	Score	Profession/job	Score
Advertising	7.3	Broadcasting	6.8

Journalism	7.5	Music	6.3
Acting	7.2	Film production	6.5
Dentistry	7.3	Doctor	6.8
Midwifery/Nursing	6.5	Pilot (civil)	7.5
Police	7.7	Ambulance service	6.3
Social work	6.0	Teaching	6.2
Mining	8.3	Construction/building	7.5

The process of change

'There is a certain relief in change, even though it be from bad to worse; as I have found in travelling in a stagecoach, that it is often a comfort to shift one's position and be bruised in a new place.' *Washington Irving*, Tales of a Traveller, *1824*

Losing your job or starting a new one, and related factors like having to move house or change location, the strain placed on relationships at home, divorce and so on, can closely mirror the symptoms of grief researched by Swiss psychiatrist Dr Elisabeth Kubler-Ross and later by Dr Eric Lindemann. Understanding this process and recognising that it is normal, affects everyone, and is relatively predictable, can help us manage our own feelings better and give us valuable empathy and insight into the feelings of others around us too.

How quickly we move through these emotions will depend on our individual circumstances of course, and we don't necessarily move through them in a straight line. It's quite common to have little relapses every now and again. A disappointment such as being turned down for a job interview can quite easily bruise us all over again, so go easy on your self. Take a quick look at the stages described below. Do any of these feelings or reactions seem familiar?

Where are you now?

Stage one – shock and denial

People who are being made redundant experience this, even if they already knew that losing their job was a possibility. A common reaction may be to deny the impact of the redundancy "This isn't (or can't) be happening to me!" It can often take some time to address the reality of what has just occurred and to take in the details of what is going to happen to you. When you've just been told that you've lost your job, it may be difficult to think about what might happen to your pension or other important details. This is why organisations making people redundant should ensure that they give them as much information as possible in writing to be read again later, and preferably a follow-up contact.

Stage two - anger

Thoughts such as "Why me?" and "It's not fair" are very common at this stage. It's really important to deal openly with what angers you about the situation and not to suppress it, so just get it off your chest. We often feel a sense of real relief after we've had a good rant (verbally or in writing) about something that makes us angry. Just remember to be sensible about it and maintain a sense of control and proportion. Although anger can de-skill you temporarily, it also creates the vital mood of self-preservation that you need to build your new life successfully.

Stage three - bargaining

This can often be a stage where you fight to keep your old job, to stop the unfortunately inevitable event. "What if I accept a pay cut?" "What if I do less hours?" Resistance may or may not be useless, however, most people will try to reduce the impact and consider other alternatives to redundancy.

Stage four – depression

Even if you hated your old job, and the end to uncertainty comes as a relief, you may well be depressed about other aspects of redundancy. Worries about money, relationships and so on are all too common at this stage. It's really important to try to act pragmatically now by sorting out your finances, registering with JobcentrePlus and dealing with any benefits you can claim, taking plenty of exercise to ward off the adverse effects of stress, and eating healthily.

Stage five - acceptance

This is the point at which you accept that your life has changed and your old one has actually gone. You'll know that this is happening when you can feel yourself saying things like "Well, I suppose if I have to deal with this (i.e. I can't resist it or rage about it any longer), then I might as well get on with it". You may also experience a willingness to look at options to move forward from redundancy and start to look at re-training, job-hunting, or perhaps setting up your own business. It's the point at which you start to go forward and use change as a catalyst for a positive outlook on life ahead and not just an obstacle to moving on to your new life.

Getting help

Talking through how we feel with friends and family can help a lot. Sometimes, however, we can't or don't want to talk to people we know about our feelings: we might prefer to talk to someone independent. In difficult times, it might also be tempting to turn to false friends like alcohol and other stimulants. The organisations and resources listed at the end of this section provide a valuable lifeline to thousands of people. There are also many things you can do to help yourself.

Additional coping strategies

- Engaging in some form of sport or exercise, especially running and swimming, help to keep us fit and release our 'feel good' hormones (endorphins), keeping us on the straight and narrow and depression at bay. So, don't be a couch potato!
- To reduce mood swings avoid caffeine, or cut down to one or two cups of coffee a day, and avoid foods high in sugar, saturated fat, salt, white flour or additives.
- Eat a balanced diet – five pieces of fruit or vegetables a day are recommended.
- Learn how to relax and breathe properly – take up yoga or Pilates.
- Avoid drugs of any kind unless they have been prescribed by your doctor.
- Try alternative remedies such as aromatherapy or Bach flower remedies.
- Try to get regular and sufficient rest. Lavender is said to have properties that induce restful sleep – a few drops of oil in your pre-bedtime bath, on your pillow, can help. Camomile or valerian tea or a mug of warm milk before bed is also relaxing. Avoid caffeine and alcohol before bedtime if you're having trouble sleeping.
- Drink alcohol in moderation or not at all.
- Maintain a positive and optimistic attitude.
- Try not to sweat the small stuff – don't worry about trivial matters.

- Have a good cry if you want to. Tears are supposed to be the 'pressure valve to the soul'. Punch a pillow – let it out.
- Be around other positive people – misery loves company and so does depression.
- Laugh and smile as often as possible during the day.
- Get plenty of hugs if you can, even if they're only from your pet.
- Try not to get upset when people say 'I know how you feel'. It's a platitude of course but they're just trying to show you they care.
- Accept the advice of others with caution. Do what you feel is best for you. Get away if you want to. Stay at home if you want to it. Whatever will genuinely help you heal and move on.
- Be prepared for set-backs. Just when you think it might all be fine and you're making headway you might feel down again. It's OK. It's normal.
- Set yourself realistic goals, write them down and check them off when you have done them to keep up a positive direction and attitude. Save the old lists to remind yourself of how much you have done or how far you have come.

Essential resources

The Samaritans, www.samaritans.org, a charity founded in 1953 by the Reverend Chad Varah, a London vicar, listens to those in emotional need in complete confidence. The Samaritans is not simply a suicide line: less than one fifth of its calls in 2005 were related to suicide. They also run a growing email service and a number of emotional health outreach projects all over Britain. Last year, Samaritans took 2.4 million phone calls, each answered by one of 17,000 people who work three or four hour shifts every four weeks.

Contact them 24 hours a day on 08457 90 90 90 (local call rate) or email jo@samaritans.org.

Alcoholics Anonymous, www.aa.org, helps those in need to deal with alcohol addiction.

Drinkline offers advice, information and support to anyone concerned about their own or someone else's drinking. Freefone 0800 917 8282.

National Drugs Helpline 24-hour helpline for drug users, their friends and families. Freefone 0800 77 66 00.

National Debtline Help for anyone in debt or concerned they may fall into debt. Call free on 0808 808 4000.

Consumer Credit Counselling (www.cccs.co.uk), free, confidential and expert advice that could help you get back on your feet and with your life. CCCS is a charity, so you won't pay a penny for any of their services - whether you need immediate debt advice tailored to your situation or more general budgeting advice.

The Citizens Advice Bureau (www.adviceguide.org.uk) has been helping people to resolve their money, legal and other problems since 1939.The website contains lots of useful information and a location directory for their branch offices.

Good reads

Who Moved my Cheese? Top-selling book on managing change in your life by Dr Spencer Johnson, Vermillion Press ISBN 0-0918-1697-1

Stress at Work, Jeremy Stranks, Elsevier Books ISBN 0-7506-6542-4

Think and Grow Rich, Napoleon Hill, The Wilshire Book Company ISBN 0-87980-163-8

Feel the Fear and Do It Anyway, Susan Jeffers, Arrow Books Ltd ISBN 0-09-974100-8

Chapter 4 Managing your time effectively

If you have been used to the routine of regular work for any length of time the sudden loss of that routine can be a mixed blessing. Common reactions can range from panic to paralysis. Putting some structure to your days as soon as possible is vital, so here are a few tips.

Job searching needs to be systematic but you shouldn't feel that you can't make some time to relax, de-stress and consider options that might take you down a new life route.

Don't forget that the **more senior a position** you are looking for, the longer the job search, interview, job offer and starting process can take. Anywhere from one month to six months from search to start date is not uncommon so you should plan to deal with the down time constructively.

You might want to consider taking on some **part-time work** to keep your hand in and bring in a bit of income, still leaving you time to go to interviews, research the market, and so on. It might lead to something more interesting and you won't be moping around in your pyjamas all day!

You could also consider doing some unpaid work in the **voluntary sector**. Chapter 17 looks at working in the not-for-profit sector. Voluntary work can help to keep your spirits up, involve you with other people, look credible on your CV and can be both genuinely rewarding and fun.

If you have a **gym membership** you've never used, now is the time to get or keep fit, and build up those endorphins generated by a brisk work-out. It might be possible to save money by downgrading to an off-peak membership if you currently have a full one. If the gym membership has had to go as a result of a new economy drive, try running, walking in a local park or favourite bit of countryside, or riding your bike. Exercise is free and a highly beneficial stress buster.

Catch up on your **reading** – start with some of the books mentioned in this one. Don't forget to fit in some fun reads too.

You could also do those things you've always said you'd do **if only you had time**. Write a list of things you have been meaning to get around to and then start ticking them off as you do them. It could be anything from sorting out the garden or fixing a dripping tap to writing your own web diary or starting the novel we all have inside us. I have made these lists a number of times and I've actually achieved a lot of the things on the list, which made me feel great. I've also discovered that I can live with some of the things I realised that no amount of free time would induce me to enjoy. Now I just don't feel guilty about not doing them. Either way, it's a result!

What about writing a **blog or a book**? You can create your own free web diary at www.blogger.com. If you want to get into writing, you could try out www.writers.com or www.writersservices.com for starters. *The Writers' & Artists' Yearbook* (A&C Black ISBN 0-7136-6936-5) is the bible on publishing for all media.

If you've always fancied setting up your own **website** or e-shop you can do it without any programming skills at very low cost these days. Lots of companies have such great economies of scale they can offer significant functionality for very low monthly fees. It's a good way to start before shelling out for a more expensive custom-made site. Chapter 12 gives more details about this.

Finances permitting, you might fancy a holiday to **give yourself a break** and get life into perspective. Do you have friends or relatives with holiday homes you might visit inexpensively? Could you do a house swap? If you're prepared to be last minute and flexible you could get just the de-stressing break you need at a bargain rate from any of the low cost airlines or travel package providers.

You may never get an opportunity like this again to take some time out and reappraise your life, so consider it a gift and use it wisely.

Chapter 5 Changing direction for new lifers

'Find a job you enjoy and you'll never work a day in your life'
Confucius

You may be reading this book because you're experiencing the void that redundancy has left in your life; or maybe you've just survived the latest corporate cull and want to get some ideas before you're next in line. Maybe you've achieved all your goals and want go to the next level, if only you knew what that might be? Perhaps you are just fed up and wonder how you ever ended up in your current job.

One of the most powerful images I ever saw to illustrate that particular point was a recruitment ad for the Royal Air Force some years ago. There was a close up of a small boy, totally absorbed in his own little fantasy world, imagining that he was a fighter pilot, using his outstretched arms as soaring wings. The caption read something like 'Because no one ever dreams of being a chartered accountant.' Well, frankly who dreams of doing most of the bizarre stuff we end up doing to earn our crust? What did you dream of being?

An optimist (and you must be one if you're reading this!) will view this as an opportunity to make changes for the better. You may or may not have had a career plan before but you're going to need one now. As your knowledge of yourself and what you want evolves, your plan will evolve with you. That's how you avoid becoming stale, cynical and stuck in a rut and avoid feeding your inner gremlins of unfulfilled need and dissatisfaction.

An Investors in People (IIP) survey revealed that an alarming number of British firms believe themselves to be populated by what is charmingly called 'dead wood'. What a waste for all concerned, but I can see why it happens. Bad jobs can be like bad marriages – people stay in them because they think there is no alternative but they don't see why they should be the one to make the first move. They're not sure if they will find anyone else, they need the money and besides the food's not so bad!

In any event, whether you were a corporate high flier in your last job or you're a job seeker with little in the way of qualifications, everyone has something to offer. Your confidence might feel a little bruised if you've been made redundant but bruises heal in time and you'll look back before long and wonder why you were ever worried about your future – because you are about to take charge of it with a vengeance.

If you are lucky enough to have been offered free outplacement or career coaching by your employer (usually provided by specialist external firms such as Penna, Right Coutts or HDA), accept it gratefully, as part of the package will usually be help in creating your new direction. There are stacks of tests out there to work out what kind of person you are and what kind of career would suit you best and by all means try a few, but the thing is *you* still have to do some hard thinking and some deciding. Tests and advisers may help but you are in charge of your own life and the direction it takes. I do, however, quite like the ones at www.tickle.com and you can take the Ocean test for free on the New Life website.

If you've been experiencing there-must-be-more-to-life-than-this syndrome, more or less the same rules apply. You can read more in the later section on exit plans and Chapter 17 on working in the not-for-profit sectors.

What do you really, really want?

This deceptively simple question generally takes quite a bit of thought or soul searching to answer. Until you have some firm conviction about it, it is hard to build a winning plan to achieve your goals, however modest or ambitious they may be. So, time thinking about what you really, really want is not a luxury, it is essential. The best ideas usually come when you're relaxed: your next brilliant brainwave might come when you're out walking the dog or making the supper, rather than while you are sitting at a desk staring at a blank sheet of paper, worrying about your credit card repayments or how much you dislike your boss. Once you have the desire to achieve your real goals you'll be unstoppable.

Never worry about the 'how' before you've figured out the 'why': you will either come up with a brilliant solution that still fails to tick all your boxes, or you'll just talk yourself out of all kinds of quite sensible (or daring) options before you've even started. Brainstorming – coming up with new ideas – relies on getting ideas down first and evaluating them objectively at a later stage.

We are so programmed to believe that we are doing the right thing if we are taking action that unfortunately we don't always stop to think – i.e. think about whether these suitable sounding jobs are in fact right for us. Will they make good use of your skills and abilities, and do they match your interests and your values? Fairly deep questions for a simple job application, I hear you say, but you will not make good career decisions if you don't ask the right questions first.

There are three important stages to developing your career plan: **understand yourself and your needs; visualise the future; write down the plan.**

Stage 1 – understand yourself

This is a so-called reflective stage where you think carefully about your motivations, interests and skills. Self-assessment will provide you with the essential information about what is important and interesting to you and is effectively an expression of your needs.

So, did your old job make you feel happy, fulfilled, challenged, completely strung out or just bored senseless?

What do you actually enjoy about work?
- the company?
- prestige?
- perks?
- money?
- admiration?
- gratitude and appreciation?
- a sense of achievement?
- intellectual challenge?
- plodding along or pushing new boundaries?
- working alone or working in a team?
- drama and gossip or a quiet life?

Most people need to work out their own combination of what I call the **7 Ps of career motivation.** You can use the 7 Ps to work out what you want and judge whether future options achieve a match or not. Your priorities can change over time, of course, and there are no right or wrong answers, only what is right for you, so be honest about your needs and desires. Don't worry about what anybody else thinks or whether it is politically correct to admit to enjoying popularity or pay rises.

- **Protection** How important is job security to you? Do you have dependants? Would a particular employer or career path offer a reasonable degree of job security? Don't forget, there is no such thing as a job for life.

- **Productivity** Do you need or like to feel very busy? Do you want the opportunity to push boundaries and be creative, or do you prefer to follow rules?
- **Prestige** Do you need an important-sounding title? A top of the range car? A corner office? The opportunity to win awards and prizes? The respect and kudos that may come from family, friends, peers, colleagues?
- **Pay** How much money do you need? How much are you worth? What other benefits would you look for? Expenses? Cars? Health care? Overtime? Bonuses? What are the opportunities to earn more?
- **Popularity** Do you need to work with a lot of people? Do you want a job that provides a social life as well? Is being liked really important to you?
- **Praise** Do you need to be thanked and recognised for your efforts more than others?
- **Promotion** Is potential for promotion important to you? Do you aspire to rise to the top of your field or be a great second-in-command or a good solid team player?

The answers to these sorts of self-assessment questions should help to make your next step easier because there is no point in going back to the kind of job where you were very unhappy. If we're being honest, that could be one of the factors that made or makes you a redundancy target in the first place.

Mapping out the things that you love or loathe about the job will help you to think about your options before you start to concern yourself with how to achieve them. For example, if you love being part of a team, will working from home on your own make you happy?

This is all concerned with finding the source of your motivation and interviewers will ask you about this so it's important to have a good and sincere response. Once you understand that you can harness it to achieve your goals because they will be linked to real desire.

Stage 2 – visualise the future

This is your chance to use your imagination to form a picture of what you want for your life and career with no constraints! So, what are your choices?

- What are your skills? Make an inventory of them.
- What are the personal qualities that make you worth employing?
- What do you really like doing?
- What can you live with? All jobs have some dull bits.
- What do you hate doing? Try to avoid jobs that include a lot of these things.
- What makes you light up with excitement and energy?
- How much time do you really want to spend at work? If you love your job you rarely question how much time you spend there.
- If you're a commuter, do you really need the extra money or could you work more locally and enjoy the time you'll save?
- How much money will you need to earn?
- Can you afford to work for free for a while to get some new experience on your CV?
- Can you afford to go part-time?
- Do you need to gain some new skills to get to where you want to go?
- Can you find some objective help to brush up your CV, interview skills or your image?
- Can you use old contacts or find new ones to help your plan along?
- Could you start your own business?

- Could you try working in your preferred field as a volunteer to see if you like it first?
- Do you like calling the shots or following a strong leader?
- Could you work as a contractor, interim manager or a freelancer?
- Be innovative: what would you do if you couldn't possibly fail?

If the answers aren't immediately clear, seem too daunting or even impossible, don't be put off. Keep at it and if you stay focused you'll be amazed at how apparent coincidences start to occur.

If you find it difficult to think about selling yourself, think of yourself in the third person and describe yourself that way (e.g. 'John is a reliable problem-solver who gets on well with his colleagues.' 'Natalie is a natural salesperson and has excellent project management skills'). It's amazing what you can say about yourself when you throw off your inhibitions (so British!) and try to see yourself objectively or as others probably see you.

If you're really serious about change and taking charge of your life you could try booking a session of Jack Black's Mindstore programme. I first met Jack, a remarkable Glaswegian, in the mid 1990s when he ran the first of his Mindstore for Business programmes. A couple of years ago, I went to one of his sessions in Kensington Town Hall. It was packed out and a staggering 35% were 'returners', people who had been not just once but several times. It's very down to earth, not expensive and he doesn't make you do anything particularly weird – but it is powerful stuff. Some of the UK's top companies and talents have been motivated by Jack to change their lives for the better – it's well worth a shot. You can check out the latest details at www.mindstore.com.

Stage 3 – write down the plan

Get yourself a notebook and be prepared for the ideas to start forming. Keep a notebook and a pen by your bedside table so you can capture the good ideas you have before going to sleep, dreaming or when you wake up. Having something written down makes you more focused, determined and purposeful.

Talk to others about your plan. It helps to clarify it in your own mind and may generate ideas and offers of help. An old colleague might give you a lead to an opportunity that would be perfect for you. Once you're not scared any more it's easy to focus and stay positive, as Susan Jeffers says in her bestselling book *Feel the Fear and Do It Anyway*.

When your plan has crystallised enough (but not before!) make sure that it includes:

- what you are actually going to do
- how you are going to do it
- when you are going to do it
- what help you will need to do it
- some idea or measure of what success will look like

Do browse the rest of this book for all the options on job hunting, business start ups, interim work, working overseas and working for a charity: it might spark off a fresh idea or two.

What now? Well, get cracking. Before you know it you will have a new life and if the feedback I get is anything to go by, it could be much better than you'd dared to hope it could be.

Career crisis exit plans

When you are made redundant the choice of whether you need to build a new life or not has already been made for you and the speed at which you need to operate to create that new life could be pretty swift. This can often lead to making ill-considered choices because panic and fear have set in as fast as your unpaid bills mount up.

Let's assume, though, that you are in employment but you just don't like what you're doing and want to make changes.

At this point, I would like to sound a note of caution.

Sometimes people want to leave their old job because they've grown out of it. They are looking for promotion rather than a completely new life. Sometimes things you don't like have happened in a job you loved, and because of a new boss, new conditions or some other irritant you may feel that you want to do something completely different.

Throwing out the baby with the bathwater and giving up a job you once loved to do something completely different, because something or somebody else spoiled it for you, may not be the best answer. You might simply need to move somewhere else to do a similar job, or to improve your skills at dealing with whatever conflicts or changes have arisen at work. This is more commonplace than people think. I come across people all the time who are planning to do the career equivalent of running off to join the circus because they haven't the skills or the confidence to change things constructively in their existing roles.

I often hear people say they want to leave their cut-throat, meaningless lives in the mammon-worshipping corporate world and down-shift or do something worthwhile. Before you burn your bridges or behave in some other lemming-like fashion you might want to take some time out to discover what that would really mean. By all means spend a holiday working in a Sri Lankan orphanage; volunteer to help in a local school if you think you fancy teaching – see if your fantasy matches your needs and desires first. If it doesn't, well you haven't lost anything. If it does – go ahead and buy all the matches you want!

The overall quality of management skills in the UK has improved enormously in recent years but there are still mountains to climb and poor management and communication is responsible for much of the discontent and frustration that prompt new lifers to look for pastures new or render them ineffective in their existing roles. This may also account for the findings of a piece of research by Rialto Consulting on the undesirability of what they have termed 'stags' in the workplace. 'Stags' are those pale, male, stale, over-40 types who apparently have neither the imagination nor the energy to perform in their jobs, who are stagnating and inhibiting the progression of the (presumably not yet cynical or burnt out) young Turks queuing up to take over their jobs and magically transform the fortunes of the company. It all sounds like wallpapering over the cracks to me. How, I wonder, do these researchers account for why such employees ended up like this in the first place?

Rennie, the indigestion tablet firm, ran a campaign to bring back the lunch break as their research indicated that one in four British workers (about 5 million people) feels pressured to forego a full lunch hour because they are worried that it gives a negative impression to colleagues and bosses. So maybe these dudes aren't stags – they simply lack energy because they're hungry!

But if none of the above applies to you and you have decided that you really want to leave your old job and go on a gap year, work abroad, train to be a plumber, run that bed & breakfast in Cornwall, set up that boutique, run your own business, etc., then you are best advised to sort out an **exit plan** while you are still employed and in a position of solvency.

So, assuming you have done your homework by consulting the other chapters in this book, the exit plan must be created and implemented properly.

Once you have new goals you may find that you have renewed vigour for all aspects of your life and not just your work.

If you have an exit plan that you have costed, and where you have laid out all the steps required in order to implement it, along with a realistic timeline, you can get started. Maybe you could start saving up or securing grants or finance, perhaps get your company to foot the bill for a bit of extra training you need, complete the admin involved in setting up your company, design your business cards at the weekends and after working hours. So, by the time you leave and shed off your old skin you can glide elegantly and seamlessly into your new life like a fully - formed butterfly instead of a slightly immature grub!

Essential resources

Think and Grow Rich, Napoleon Hill, The Wilshire Book Company ISBN 0-87980-163-8

Feel the Fear and Do It Anyway, Susan Jeffers, Arrow Books Ltd ISBN 0-09-974100-8

Anyone Can Do It – 57 Real-life Laws on Entrepreneurship, Sahar and Bobby Hashemi, Capstone ISBN 1-84112-204-1

Career break new lifers

It doesn't matter whether you're returning to the world of paid or unpaid work outside the home after a few months or several years, whatever the reason – maternity leave, children growing up and away, serious illness, divorce and so on – going back to work and building a new life can feel scary.

Whether you were a corporate high flier or you're a mature job seeker with little in the way of recent experience, everyone has their own issues, which can include a general lack of confidence and uncertainty about the currency of skills, knowledge or contacts. Everyone has something to offer – modesty may be your greatest virtue but it can be your Achilles' heel in these situations.

Career breakers often need to create new lives to fit with their current circumstances, not to mention the different priorities and values that having children, or changed family circumstances, often bring. More and more women are setting up their own very successful businesses because they find it either difficult or just plain unappealing to break back into the mainstream job market. A career break can sometimes become a permanent fracture.

In any event, before you write off your chances of success or plunge into an interview completely unprepared, so that failure becomes a self-fulfilling prophecy, take some time out to think about the questions about changing direction outlined earlier in this section.

What do you really, really want?

Consider the additional issues that particularly affect returners.

- How much time do you really want spend at work?
- Can you go part-time initially and build up gradually?
- Is commuting viable or not?
- How will your childcare arrangements work?
- Do you need to brush up on a few skills first? Some industries run back to work training programmes particularly in SET (Science, Engineering & Technology), your local college or professional body may be able to help.
- How much money will you need to earn to make it worthwhile?
- Can you get some help to brush up your CV, interview skills or your image?
- Can you use old contacts or find new ones to help your plan?
- Can you rely on a partner's income while building up a new business or study path?

Once again, if the answers aren't immediately clear or seem too daunting or impossible, don't be put off. Keep at it and if you stay focused you will be amazed at how coincidence starts to grow. Talk to others about your plan. It helps to clarify it in your own mind and may generate ideas and offers of help. A neighbour might tell you about a great crèche or an old colleague might give you a lead to a vacancy they think would be perfect for you.

There is a lot more help and advice around for career returners than there ever was, so my advice is, take it and make it yours!

Essential resources

Here some useful resources for returners. Don't forget to look at the other sections of this book on business start up, working in the voluntary sector and so on.

www.women-returners.co.uk A charity helping women returners – does what it says on the tin!

www.ncwgb.org The National Council of Women (NCW) conducts research on women's issues. Branches nationwide.

www.womens-institute.org.uk The National Federation of Women's Institutes (NFWI) is the largest voluntary organisation for women in Britain.

www.dressforsuccess.org Dress for Success is an international charity providing appropriate clothing for low-income women returners.

www.motheratwork.co.uk A total resource site for working mothers.

www.homeworking.com Advice for home workers, including scam reports.

www.netmums.com Local info sites run by mums for mums.

www.prowess.org.uk A Trade Association for organisations committed to providing women-friendly business support.

www.bawe-uk.org British Association for Women Entrepreneurs (BAWE).

www.earlyyearsonline.co.uk A directory of validated childcare providers, holiday clubs, etc.

Diana Wolfin and Susan Foreman have written a really excellent book called *Back to Work – A Guide for Women Returners*, ISBN 1-86105-588-9. It's full of top tips and help and worth £9.99 of anyone's money. Diana has acres of experience in this field and can be contacted via her website **www.changingdirection.com**.

Chapter 6 Job-hunting

'Take care to get the job you like; otherwise you will have to like the job you get.' *Anon*

When you know you're about to lose the job you've got, it's important to start gearing up for your next one, if that's what you really want. Make sure, however, that you have done as suggested in Chapter 5 and taken some time to really think about what you want before you start hunting. Recruiters will be able to tell if you don't really know what you want and you'll make difficult or impossible for them to help you.

In this chapter I'll be pointing you in the right direction to get help for writing or updating your CV, how to go about your search and interview advice.

If, however, building a new life by working for yourself is more appealing, turn to the chapters in this book on being your own boss. If you are fed up with the corporate world and fancy a shot at working in the not-for-profit sector, check out Chapter 17. Maybe you want to think about a complete career change, retrain to do something else or brush up your existing skills? If so, go to Chapter 15 on re-training or coaching. It may be an unpalatable thing to consider, but if you think that your old job became at risk because of a skills deficit that could become a barrier to your success, give careful consideration to plugging that gap before you start applying for new jobs.

If you have been lucky enough to be offered outplacement by your employer, an objective skills assessment may well be part of the deal. If not, coaches can be very useful in this regard – you can find out more about them in Chapter 18. Friends or former colleagues may well be able to help too. Ask them by all means but if they give you feedback you don't like, don't blame them for giving you what you were looking for and get all defensive. Giving constructive feedback is based on trust and objectivity and it is not a skill that everyone has mastered. Many feel uncomfortable about it, especially if they think it may jeopardise their relationship with you. So treat them gently and listen carefully and calmly!

Top tips for job hunting

- If your employer has offered you outplacement services, grab them with both hands!
- Sometimes it's a buyer's market, sometimes it's a seller's market; either way you need a job so get out there and fight for one, don't sit around in your pyjamas waiting for one to appear out of thin air.
- Determine your job goals, write them down and then focus your efforts towards them.
- Use the internet to help organise your search – the New Life website features all the top job boards and recruiters – all in one convenient place.
- Use every available resource – internet, networking, job fairs, recruitment agencies, temp agencies, direct approaches. Don't presume that the only companies with vacancies are the employers who are advertising where you happen to look.
- Use your networks of friends and family to find permanent or temporary work.
- *Executive Grapevine* is the bible for researching Executive Search Firms – see if your library or your HR department has a copy as it's too expensive for individual purchase. There is a list of the top ones on the New Life website.
- Don't just consider the big companies: 95% of all organisations in the UK are SMEs (small and medium enterprises) with 250 or fewer employees.

- Keep a spreadsheet or a record of passwords and user ID names so you don't waste time getting locked out of bookmarked sites on the internet – you can download a free template on the New Life website.
- If you don't have home access to the internet (preferably broadband), check out access at your local Job Centre or an internet cafe.
- Save money on newspapers – check job pages in your local library.
- Think about who can or will act as a referee for you and sound them out in advance if possible.
- Turn up to interviews on time, calm, prepared and well-groomed.
- Remember first impressions count – a smile, a firm confident handshake and good manners.
- **The Big Three.** Interviews usually revolve around three questions:
  - o 1 Can you do the job? This tests skill, experience and track record.
  - o 2 Will you do the job? This tests motivation, commitment and enthusiasm.
  - o 3 Will you fit in? This tests your cultural fit with others.
- Don't accept any old offer that comes along, unless you are really desperate.
- Save questions about salary and benefits for when they are making you an offer, not before.
- Put in plenty of effort: job hunting can be a bit of a numbers game.
- Keep a thorough record of all your applications, status, follow ups, interview dates, etc. (you will need this if you are claiming Jobseekers Allowance).
- If you get downhearted, get it off your chest and confide in a trusted friend.
- If you get an offer make sure you read the tips on starting a new job later on in the book.

- Don't expect a reply to every letter you send – this sort of politeness just isn't an industry standard.
- Many search consultants are excellent, many are not – don't take it personally!
- Remember, search consultants work for the company who hires them not for the candidate.
- Search consultants are usually paid a percentage of your proposed salary as their fee, which is why they will get you the best deal possible and need you to stay at least six months in a post.
- Many recruitment firms are little more than CV farms with online databases using key word searches so make sure your CV contains the right key words for the job you want so it will come up on database searches.
- Try and meet the recruiters – it helps them to remember you better and build commitment.
- Keep your CV regularly updated, especially if you take on any relevant voluntary work or study.

Essential resources

A brilliant book on this topic is *Great Answers to Tough Interview Questions* by Martin John Yate, published by Kogan Page ISBN 0-7494-4356-1: well worth the £8.99 cover price.

The New Life website features a simple directory of all the top job boards and recruiters so make it your first stop, however, here are a few to start you off.

www.totaljobs.com A general recruitment site.

www.fish4.co.uk According to them, the UK's most visited recruitment site.

www.monster.co.uk A general recruitment site.

www.jobcentreplus.gov.uk Government recruitment site. The Job Centre will steer you to this. Fine for local work, minimum wage-type vacancies and public sector jobs but not for serious commercial positions.

www.worktrain.gov.uk Government site with details of job and learning opportunities.

www.workthing.com A general recruitment site.

Women checking out attractive employers may want to visit the Aurora website first: **www.WhereWomenWantToWork.com**

Executive and senior managerial resources

They all say they are the leading one. Well, who cares, as long as they are prepared to help you and treat you with respect? Executive Grapevine publishes a market share table every year for the top 10 search companies. I have annotated their rankings and market share after their entry in brackets. It doesn't change much so this is still pretty accurate.

Top 10 search companies

- Spencer Stuart **www.spencerstuart.com** (rank 1; market share 5.9%)
- Odgers Ray & Berndtson **www.odgers.com** (rank 2; market share 5.8%)
- Whitehead Mann **www.wmann.com** (rank 3; market share 5.5%)
- Russell Reynolds **www.russellreynolds.com** (rank 4; market share 5.4%)

- Egon Zehnder International **www.egonzehnder.com** (rank 5; market share 5.0%)
- Heidrick & Struggles **www.heidrick.com** (rank 6; 4.1% market share 4.1%)
- Korn Ferry **www.ekornferry.com** (rank 7; market share 3.9%)
- Harvey Nash **www.harveynash.com** (rank 8; market share 1.9%)
- Hogarth Davies Lloyd **www.hdl.co.uk** (rank 9; market share 1.7%; deal exclusively with finance vacancies)
- Sheffield Howath **www.sheffieldhaworth.com** (rank 10; market share 1.6% deal exclusively with finance vacancies)

Other executive resources

www.eotn.co.uk Execs on the net. Provides a selection of executive appointments and interims.

www.timesonline.co.uk/appointments The *Times*, excellent line managerial job search service. The Tuesday edition of the newspaper has a special section on public sector jobs. The *Times Educational Supplement* is great for, funnily enough, jobs in education.

www.jobs.telegraph.co.uk/ The *Daily Telegraph*, excellent line managerial job search service. On Thursdays the paper has a special over-£55K jobs section.

http://jobs.guardian.co.uk The *Guardian*, search by sector or by employer. Dominant in public sector, education, media, graduate and permanent IT positions. Includes a useful career manager.

Public sector specialists

www.veredus.co.uk Veredus, part of the Capita Group

www.tribalresourcing.com Tribal Resourcing

It is worth noting that the public sector usually has a rather different recruitment process approach to that of the private sector if you are moving from one to the other. You will normally be given very strict guidelines on the construction of your application and you must be prepared to supply references up front who may well be asked to comment before you are made an offer, so be careful who you nominate. In addition, you may have to be interviewed on the same day along with your competitors. Offers are often made on the day or at least very shortly after. In many ways, it is much more efficient than the drawn out, 'free for all' which is all too common in the private sector. It doesn't necessarily mean they are any better at hiring quality candidates, they just don't mess you about as much!

Industry sector specialist recruitment sites

Jobs in agriculture and the green industry
www.bloominggoodjobs.com
www.jobs.co.uk/agriculturejobs/

Jobs in accounting and finance
www.accountancyagejobs.com
www.gaapweb.com
www.totallyfinancial.com
www.cityjobs.co.uk

http://accounting.topjobs.co.uk
www.jobs1.co.uk

Jobs in IT
www.computingcareers.co.uk
www.computerweekly.com
www.cwjobs.co.uk
www.jobs1.co.uk

Jobs in the medical profession
www.nursefindersuk.com
www.jobs1.co.uk
www.nurserve.co.uk
www.bna.co.uk
www.nettingtheevidence.org.uk
www.medicallocumjobs.com
www.jobsinmedicine.co.uk
www.emedcareers.co.uk medical sales jobs

Jobs in HR
www.mdh.co.uk
www.inhr.co.uk
www.personneltoday.com
www.jobs4hr.com
www.cpdrecruitment.com

Jobs in construction
www.jobsinconstruction.co.uk
www.constructor.co.uk
www.jobs.co.uk/constructionjobs
www.justconstruction.net

Jobs in hotels and catering
www.myrestaurantjob.co.uk
www.caterer.com
www.hcareers.co.uk

http://catering.topjobs.co.uk
www.hotel-jobs.co.uk
www.luxuryhoteljobs.com
www.finediningjobs.com
www.hotrecruit.co.uk

Jobs in secretarial and admin
www.secrecruit.co.uk
http://www.vedior.com
http://jobs.reed.co.uk
www.secsinthecity.co.uk

Jobs in retailing
www.retailchoice.com
www.thegrocer.co.uk
www.inretail.co.uk
www.allretailjobs.com
www.talismanretail.co.uk
www.jobopenings.net

Jobs in the legal profession
www.lawcrossing.co.uk
www.totallylegal.com
www.ten-percent.co.uk
www.lawrecruiter.co.uk

Jobs in the beauty, spa and leisure industry
www.hairandbeautyjobs.com
www.rsr-solutions.co.uk
www.activeconnection.co.uk

Jobs in the motor trade and logistics
www.onlinecarjobs.co.uk Mechanics, sales, garages
www.bsm.co.uk British School of Motoring
www.clear-stone.co.uk HGV specialists
www.manpower.co.uk All driving jobs

Jobs in call centres
www.hotrecruit.co.uk
www.teleresources.co.uk
http://call-centre.topjobs.co.uk

Jobs in the media and advertising
www.mediabistro.com
www.recruitmedia.co.uk
www.massmediajobs.com
www.creativepool.co.uk
http://uk.music-jobs.com
www.dmjobs.co.uk Direct marketing jobs
www.productionbase.co.uk
www.film-tv.co.uk
www.simplymarketingjobs.co.uk

About recruitment consultants

There are lots of different types of **recruitment consultant** out there. Essentially they make their money from the company that is looking to hire someone. They may be paid a flat fee or a percentage of the final package they negotiate for a successful candidate. If they're lucky they are paid a retainer by certain firms but that is fairly rare these days.

So, it stands to reason that they will make more effort to hire a finance director on £100,000 per annum at, for example, a 20% fee than someone applying for a low paid admin job. It also explains why they will try their best to get you the most advantageous pay and benefits deal.

For that money, however, the company will expect certain things. There are two basic reasons why employers commission external recruiters.

- To save them time – by refining shortlists and only sending along suitable candidates for further interviews.
- And/or because they have inside knowledge and access to the best candidates.

For that reason it pays to know which recruitment agencies specialise in your type of work because it is more likely that they will attract the best vacancies from the best companies. General recruitment agencies may have lots of volume but they often lack specialist industry knowledge that allows them to understand what **you** have to offer and help you to exploit it correctly. That is why some agencies are known dismissively in the trade as 'CV farms' – they don't add a lot of value and probably don't offer candidates much of a service but they still charge high fees. I remember using one particular consultant a few years ago who sent me several candidates for a position for which I was recruiting. Two of the candidates happened to let slip that they had never met the consultant in question nor had they even gone through a telephone interview. In fact, the consultant hadn't really told them what the job was about. I wondered why they had even turned up. Needless to say it wasn't a productive experience for me or the candidates, nor did I ever use that consultant again.

Executive search firms usually employ researchers to go out and look for candidates against a specific brief so while it never hurts to be known to them, simply sending in a CV and hoping that they will be sitting on the right job for you won't usually work. It is a system that favours the employed, of course. Savvy receptionists usually know when researchers are calling to get the names of their star performers and are often taught how to foil them. Certain researchers call me at regular intervals to see if I know anyone who might fit a particular bill or to check out a particular name that they have been given elsewhere. If you were to receive a call from them because someone has recommended you they will never divulge their sources.

Good executive recruiters are worth their weight in gold but there are those who give the industry a bad name. For example: if they ask you to agree to be considered for a position and then don't call you if you fail to make it to the next stage; if they don't know or share the full interview process with you; if they don't know who the players are or can't add any value beyond a job description; if when you've been down to the final two or three and then they don't call to thank you or commiserate with you, they generally don't understand simple manners or the basic rules of professionalism. Many people have told me that although they have made no complaint about the recruiter in question at the time, if they were to be in a position to put business their way in the future, they would not do so.

Generally there will be a claw back or refund clause in their contract which means they need a candidate to stay in a job for a particular length of time, usually linked to probation periods, so it is in their interest that you stay. For that reason they should usually call you once you have started your new job to see how you're settling in.

Outplacement

It never pays to assume that everyone knows what you're talking about, and I was prompted by a message from a visitor to the New Life website that clearly underlined that point. 'What exactly is outplacement?' he asked.

As I have acknowledged in earlier parts of the book, when you are suddenly called into the office and told that your services are no longer required, it can be very difficult to think about what it is you are going to do next. Involuntary unemployment can upset carefully managed career plans and face you with the prospect of having to leave the only thing you'd ever considered doing. One of the best things that you can do is to make sure that you are offered an outplacement service as part of the package

There are a variety of firms, both large and small, that provide **outplacement services** to organisations making redundancies. What they provide, how they provide it and how long they provide it for, are usually subject to the contract your former employer has established with them. The more generous the contract, the more generous the service will be.

Sometimes you can choose your own provider but usually you are directed to the company's choice of partner. Essentially, the company is paying for professional help to get redundant employees back on their feet again as quickly as possible. Not all organisations provide this free help. Not all can afford it, as it doesn't come cheaply. So, it isn't necessarily the case that your erstwhile employer doesn't care about your future well-being, they simply may not be able to run to paying the bill for it. Some may have other, more colourful, explanations as to why their former bosses aren't helping them in this way, but calling in an outplacement provider when you've called in the receivers, is not always an option (unless you were part of the Rover Group!).

However, according to **Right Coutts**, one of the big players in this market, one of the key reasons for employers providing outplacement is that it has a clear positive impact on the **organisation's reputation** among **remaining employees**, the wider community in which it operates and the job market in general. This is of course of significant interest to the **investor**

community and **the media** as well. Outplacement is not, however, just about systems, processes and facilities. Research from HR consultancy Penna on outplacement purported to prove that the real value is the personal connection between an individual and the assigned coach.

Essentially most outplacement providers will provide a mixture of the following:

- career counselling, profiling, individualised assessment of potential and strengths
- CV advice
- counselling on issues such as finances or emotional responses to redundancy, a shoulder to cry on if you don't succeed at an interview
- access to job searching tools: the internet, recruitment directories, newspapers, etc.
- access to CV production tools: computers with word processing software, printers, etc.
- seminars on options such as starting your own business, etc.
- help with networking
- access to other people in the same boat as you – share your ups and downs, tips and helpful resources

The important thing to realise about these services is that it is still down to you to do the work. They will not apply for jobs for you and they will not arrange interviews for you. Recruitment companies can do that and so can you. It is up to you and your own efforts but they will give you every support and guidance so that you are as well placed as possible to get that important job you always really wanted.

Networking

Mention the word **networking** and most Brits will be rushing for cover. Talking to complete strangers? Touting for work? Advertising your jobless status? Most people would rather bite off their own limbs than have to endure what they might consider to be the ultimate indignity after a veritable tsunami of other employment-related suffering.

Well, dislike the idea as you may, networking is vital when it comes to finding a new job or building up a client portfolio if you're going to go down the consulting route. Our American cousins seem to have few inhibitions when it comes to such matters. They generally view our modesty and reserve with bewilderment. Still, you don't have to have your teeth whitened, your face fixed in a dazzling smile, or need to change your nationality to be a successful networker, but you do need to have **faith in yourself**, what you have to offer and the goodwill of others. By the way, networking is a two-way process, if you are just out for yourself, not what you might be able to do for others it probably won't do you any long-term good.

Personally, I am a very reluctant salesperson if it comes to something I don't believe or have pride in, so I don't do it. Well, that or I battle away to change to my satisfaction whatever it is that has got in my way of being able to move forward. However, when I find myself having to sell or talk about something I like, feel passionate about, am proud of and believe in, then I'm comfortable, persuasive and generally successful. And you can be too.

So, if you **hate networking** ask yourself, 'What's my problem?' Are you shy? Embarrassed? Lacking confidence? Once you can be honest enough with yourself about the root cause of your reticence or reluctance, you can get on with overcoming it and moving on.

Top tips for networking

- Avoid being phoney and avoid other phonies. Most people can smell insincerity a mile off.
- You might need some help, of course, a friend or a trusted adviser to deal with your issues so make sure you find someone to talk to and coach you.
- Sometimes you just need that first spark of **courage** to make that first telephone call, write that first letter, make that first move.
- Once you gain some confidence, keep going until you get what you want.
- You can live off the warm glow a successful contact can give you for a while and use it to find others.
- Know what you want, stay focused about getting it and don't be afraid to ask. The worst thing that anyone can say is 'no'. It's not like asking for directions in your car!
- If one person can't help you, when they warm to you, they can often put you in touch with someone else they know who can help you.
- Remember, the difference between a warm lead and a cold one can be significant – so get the heating on!
- Don't be afraid to cite others: 'Bob (or whoever) said I should speak to you' – as long as he actually did.
- There are many network groups out there but you need to be choosy.
- Look carefully for what you get for your money: news, networking opportunities, ads on a website, the ability to post notices, a newsletter or magazine, cheap conferences, discounts you can use in your business, e.g. insurance, social events, etc.

- Try to go to initial meetings for free as a guest if you can, before you pay any subscriptions.
- Try networking opportunities first. You will often halve the number of groups to which you belong by the time the renewal period comes around.
- Even when you get a new job you might want to keep in touch – you could help someone else who is wearing your old jobless shoes.
- Always remember to take plenty of business cards to networking events – hand them out and collect them from other people. Then follow them up!
- Even if you don't have a business to put on your card, have some cards with your contact details and key skill areas on to hand out. You can get them made very inexpensively on the internet but do make sure that they are decent quality and sell you effectively.

Finding places to network

There are plenty of networking groups around. There are specialist groups for businesswomen, those organised by the local Chambers of Commerce and Trade Associations with local chapters (e.g. Chartered Institute of Marketing (CIM), Chartered Institute of Management (CMI), Chartered Institute of Professional Development (CIPD)) and college alumni associations. Your local Business Link contact will probably know many that are local to your area or employment specialism if you need some ideas. Some commercial networking groups like Business Network International (BNI) charge significant fees but are very active – just pick those that suit you and you can feel comfortable with.

How to write an impressive CV

There are seemingly a trillion books on CV writing, lots of advice on different websites, and so on, and you will find a few ideas in the top tips section later on. However, lots of site visitors have asked for no-nonsense advice on it so I decided that it merited a little more attention in this book. There's also a free CV template that you can download at www.newlifenetwork.co.uk/.

Sometimes you may have to fill in an application form (and/or medical forms, diversity surveys, etc.) that the organisation supplies as well as providing your own CV. You must fill these forms in exactly according to their instructions and preferably ask for an electronic version so that you can type your responses into it directly.

You have to see your CV as your key piece of sales literature about yourself. If the people interviewing you already know you they may not be quite so finicky about the layout and so on but when complete strangers (like recruitment consultants, HR staff, the recruiting manager, other interested parties) look at your CV they have to be able to see something about you that makes them want to select you for a short-list and, if you are successful, an interview and a job offer.

A CV leaves a trail of clues that the recruiter will look for to confirm whether you should be included or excluded from their current job brief. You should make it easy for them to pick you, especially as there might be a large number of applicants and it must be able to tell your story after the interview is over. You can subject the finished article to the **AIDA** test – something those with a marketing training will recognise as it is used for vetting the effectiveness of advertising copy.

AIDA stands for:

- **Attention** Will your CV grab the initial attention of the recruiter or the search engine? Is it 'specifically vague' – specific enough to gain their attention while being enticing enough for them to want to know more about you? Many recruitment databases use keywords for selection, so make sure your CV contains the keywords for the positions you want to be selected for, e.g. particular programming languages, skills, job titles, etc.
- **Interest** Will your CV hold their interest? Does it have substance?
- **Desire** Will your CV make people want to shortlist you? Talk to you? Interview you?
- **Action** Will they make an appointment to see you? Recommend you to others in the recruiting chain?

How long should my CV be?

There is a view that a CV should be no longer than two sides of A4. Now, that is perfectly fine for new graduates, young people, those who haven't done much or moved around at all. If you are more experienced and older, then three pages or, at most, two double-sided sheets of A4 should be fine. The point is that it must contain quality information about you relative to the position for which you are applying. Two sides of A4 covered in badly articulated rubbish full of spelling mistakes and inaccuracies will not get you anywhere. A certain amount of gilding the lily is commonplace on CVs but the information must be essentially accurate and truthful as you could have any offer withdrawn if you are proved to have lied or deliberately misled your employer later on in the process.

So, when considering your CV there are some **basic items** that must be included and some optional extras and methodologies. Always include:

- Your full name (spelled out, not initials).
- Your contact address, usually your home address, including the postcode.
- Your telephone numbers: day, evening, mobile.
- Your email address: the one you will use for correspondence. (Employers can look at your email traffic so don't send or receive mail you wouldn't want them to know about).
- Any relevant letters after your name – qualifications, professional or trade initials.
- Your education record – places and dates with qualifications gained and levels (new graduates may find that they need to put this in detail, those with 20 years' experience can get away with the number of O levels without specifying topics or grades, the number and topics of A levels; any NVQs or certificates, the level, title and grade of higher educational awards, e.g. BA (Hons) 2:2 English Literature). If you are currently studying for a new qualification but have not yet completed it, add it in with the appropriate wording and a projection of your achievement. You always put your IT skills in here too even if you just say 'computer literate – proficient in (for example) Microsoft Word, Excel, PowerPoint, Outlook, etc.'

Additional information

- A line to state that you are entitled to work in the country, EU, etc., provided you are. You will be asked to provide proof of residency or a passport before an offer is made as a matter of course these days.

- Driver's licence – add 'full' and 'clean' if it is!
- Languages spoken and fluency in each.
- Date of birth (optional on a CV but will normally have to be divulged if an offer is made).
- A simple one- or two-line summary at the beginning summing up what you are, e.g. 'Bob Baker is a highly experienced change management consultant, specialising in the financial services sector.' Don't fill it with jargon or meaningless superlatives. A lot of consultants don't like these but some do so try it out and if it doesn't work get rid of it.

Additional options

- Information about your past training record – what courses you have been on – shows whether you and/or your employer have invested in your skills.
- Any extras you may deem relevant to demonstrate leadership, teamwork or drive such as voluntary work, being a speaker at trade conferences, captaining the company football team, being part of a mentoring set up, winning a top performance award, where and how a gap year was spent, etc.
- Be careful of including hobbies. Sometimes these are important to the job. Salespeople who can play golf may consider that hobby to be an asset but you may want to keep your love of train spotting and collection of Toby jugs to yourself! If it's an asset, add it, if not, omit it.

Career summary

If you have had a number of jobs make sure it is easy for the reader to see exactly when you held the job, which company it was for, where you were located, to whom you were responsible, and your job title. You could put in a short summary at the beginning so the recruiter can see your career at a glance. Again, some like this approach and some don't. Make sure any significant gaps are accounted for because most interviewers will ask you what you were doing.

Date	Company	Position held	Location	Reporting to
Jan 2003 – April 2005	Tescobury's	Branch Manager	Luton	Regional Director – South

Then add your key achievements: these need to be punchy and pertinent. They can be written in bullet point style, and should definitely not be written like an essay. You should pick up on words mentioned in the ad to which you are replying. If they want someone with a lot of experience managing change or project management, make sure you home in on those achievements. This sort of focus will win you an interview or make sure you are picked up on a recruiter's database search engine. You can tell them about all your other wonderful achievements later on if necessary.

Don't be over-modest: if you increased the company sales by 20%, say so. If you delivered your projects on time and to budget, say so. If you achieved all your targets three years in a row, say so. If you are one of a few people in the industry to achieve a prestigious award, say so. People want to know what you did for your previous employers to see if you could make valuable contributions to their own organisation. In other words they want evidence of your past performance to use as an indicator of your future performance. It doesn't always follow: the so-called Peter Principle is based on people being promoted to a level where they can't cope and then spending the rest of their lives hanging on for dear life. Recognise that, anyone?

Format

- Most computerised recruitment databases will only accept Microsoft Word documents so make sure yours is configured in an acceptable format. It is unlikely that you will be able to submit anything with flashy graphics or colours because it will take up too much storage.

- Fonts should be kept the same throughout – stick to contemporary types that look good both printed out and on computer screens, such as Arial or Verdana. A 10- or 12-point font size is the norm.
- If you are emailing your CV directly to a recruiter for a specific job by all means use colour to bring out text and headings if you must but don't go overboard.

- Get someone else to go through your CV and tidy it up if needs be – and always run it through a spell check.

- If you need to post a hard copy of your application (increasingly rare nowadays with so much communication by email) print it on to good quality, plain cream or white paper (better for photocopying). If you are applying for a wacky job with a quirky employer by all means turn it into a paper aeroplane, print on multicoloured paper and tell them about your penchant for extreme sports such as ironing shirts suspended over a glacier. Normal people applying for normal jobs with most rather conservative employers can just stay with the basics and will probably end up with an offer just the same!

Covering letters

If your CV has been picked up by a recruiter from a database you may never need to write a covering letter. However, if you apply for a job directly you will need to attach one either in hard copy, attached to your CV, or as an email with your CV as an attachment. You have the opportunity to offer a summary about why you have applied for the job and why they should be bothering to read your CV. Employers like well-motivated people who are efficiency minded, profit oriented and want to add value in return for their benefits package, so this is your chance to appeal to their needs directly and show that you have read and understood their job advertisement. Keep it short, punchy and polite.

Top tips for preparing a CV

- Prepare your CV so that it is ready to send out as soon as you spot an opportunity.
- Make sure your CV sells you and your achievements – this is no time for modesty.
- Create one core CV and adapt it to the individual positions you are applying for.
- Save each version with a clear naming rationale you can identify for reference purposes later, e.g. job title/company/date or marketingmanager/company nameplc/12.12.09
- Sending CVs and applications by email saves money on postage and is much faster.
- Write a punchy covering letter to go with your CV tailored to each job opportunity.

- A two-page CV is suitable for younger, less experienced people. A maximum of four pages is usually OK for more seasoned applicants, as long as it isn't padded with waffle.

Interview questions usually revolve around the Big Three so make sure your CV answers the questions: Can you do the job? Will you do the job? Will you fit in?

- Make sure your CV contains the right key words for the job you want so it will come up on database searches.
- Keep your CV regularly updated, especially if you take on any relevant voluntary work or study.
- Updating a CV can often result in renewed interest from recruiters.
- Get help on your CV from trusted friends, recruiters, or even a paid professional.
- Think about who will act as a referee for you and sound them out in advance if possible.

Essential resources

'Why You? CV messages to win jobs' by John Lees, McGraw Hill, ISBN 13-978-007711510-4

Your personal image – looking good, feeling great

I make no secret of the fact that I am a big fan of Trinny and Susannah of former *What Not to Wear* fame. I don't much care for the way they bully and pull people around but the positive transformations they make to their victims' appearance and confidence is undeniable. Those who are prepared to pooh-pooh the importance of looking good as shallow conceit should carefully reconsider their position when it comes to surviving in the job market.

In today's politically correct climate we are not supposed to give any credence to the fact that people can be and are routinely discriminated against because of their appearance – I'm not talking about race here, by the way. People with poor posture and grooming can appear lacking in the confidence and perhaps gravitas that those who can make or break our futures consider to be appropriate for the matters in hand. Richard Branson may have broken the mould of the formula suit = success, but he is always well groomed and has enough presence to sink a battleship, not to mention the money to call his own shots of course. Dress-down codes at work have been abandoned in many firms wishing to be progressive because it broke down structures and cultures in ways that they were neither prepared for nor comfortable with. You are always being watched and judged by someone, whether you like it or not!

Clothes matter. Clothes send non-verbal signals to others about our competence and trustworthiness and how well we fit into a group. Imagine visiting a hospital to find that your surgeon was dressed like a youngster in a skateboarding park or had the personal hygiene of a tramp? We may not consider that we wear a uniform for work if we are not members of the armed forces, the police or an AA patrolman but actually we do – our suits, our chinos and polo shirts, our faded jeans and jacket combos, they are all uniforms of a sort.

So, appearance is important when it comes to keeping your job *and* getting a new one. If you are highly competent but look frayed and worn out, you might not compare well with a person who is better turned out but not necessarily as experienced as you, nor as good at the job. So if one of you has to be chosen for redundancy, promotion or a new job, which one of you has the edge? Of course it isn't quite as simple as that but I'm trying to illustrate the point that you need to use **all** the tools at your disposal in the survival game. This isn't about beauty parades; it's about the communication of reliability, intelligence, trustworthiness, competence, leadership, teamwork and consideration of others. You might need to create a smart impression at an interview to get the job or a promotion even if you don't need to wear smart attire once you start the job. Bank managers and customers usually require us to pay attention to our appearance too if we seriously want them to lend us money or buy our products or services.

Top tips for improving image

- **Personal grooming matters**

  - *Hair*
    - A good, *flattering* hair cut takes years off. A good hairdresser or barber is worth their weight in gold.
    - Avoid bad home perms or colours or untouched roots. Better grey than the odd ginger hue that poorly applied dyes can create in artificial light.
    - Clean, healthy looking, no dandruff, not too much gel or styling product.
    - No extreme styles if the work environment doesn't warrant it.
  - Eyebrows frame the face – for women they must be naturally shaped and for men, try to avoid that sprouting, Dennis Healey antler look that seems to happen to the over-40s.
  - Facial hair is still considered taboo for men in many jobs and definitely for women (electrolysis is relatively inexpensive or use Jolen bleach). Men must shave properly; change the blade in the

razor regularly and shave with the line of the hair not against it to avoid razor burn and cuts.

o Clean, well-trimmed nails, no vivid polish for women, keep artificial nails natural looking and not so long that you can't do your job. There should be no nicotine stains on fingers either.

o As far as make-up goes, less is more for most women. I once read that women who wear well-applied, subtle make-up earn more. Who knows? It's got to be worth a shot though. The nightclub look definitely doesn't do for women who aspire to be taken seriously. Many beauty salons offer make up lessons that are well worth the money and you can get a free makeover at most of the top department store beauty counters.

o Fragrance – light colognes on either gender are fine, overpowering, cheap ones can seriously offend. Wear fragrance-free anti-perspirant or deodorant – it's better for your clothes anyway. Never smell of alcohol and preferably not of smoke either. Our sense of smell is one our most powerful and evocative senses.

* *Clothing*

o For women – moderation in all things, not too much cleavage or leg or anything else for that matter on show. The more skin you show the less professional you appear.

o For men – no workman's butt cleavage or beer gut on show or peeping through a shirt.

o A good, classic, well-cut suit in a serviceable fabric really makes a man look the part at work or at an interview. Better to have a few well-cut suits in basic navy and charcoal and ring the changes with shirts and ties than lots of cheap items. Suits don't need to be dry-cleaned too often either. Marks can be carefully sponged off (or use dry cleaning wipes for small stains especially on ties, available from department stores like John Lewis and M&S). Always keep suits well pressed and once the trousers are shiny, discard them. Better still, you could buy one jacket with two pairs of trousers. If formal suits aren't part of the dress culture of the firm you work for or aspire to work for a jacketed outfit may be suitable. Make sure the weights of the fabrics and colours tone properly. Certainly no character ties or socks if you want to be taken seriously and no fancy coloured socks either, stick to black and navy. Black shoes, in classic styles should be well polished. Don't spoil a good suit by wearing an unsuitable anorak type jacket over the top in winter; buy a proper coat or a light raincoat.

o   If you have or want a funky job in a fashion store, hairdresser or an advertising agency by all means wear what is appropriate. Just make sure it doesn't scare the customers.

o   Women don't have to wear butch, mannish suits to carry off an air of confidence or authority at work. Good quality fabric, well-cut items that flatter, good shoes and bags are available in most high street stores these days. Buy the best quality items you can afford and look after them properly.

o   De-clutter your wardrobe regularly. If you haven't worn something for three years or more give it to a charity shop. If something can clearly be identified as a 1980s power suit complete with shoulder pads, save it for fancy dress!

o Keep buttons sewn on properly, zips repaired, hems up, shoes polished and heeled, sweaters de-bobbled and suits free of lint and pet hair.

o Black can appear very austere so unless you're applying for a job in a funeral home or it's the company uniform, stick to dark classics like navy and charcoal for men and perhaps other dark colours like plum, teal and dark brown for women.

* *Accessories*
   o Women don't sport matching bags and shoes any more but the bags and shoes you use should at least complement each other.
   o Keep jewellery to classic basics and steer away from novelty items, especially for interviews. Watch and wedding ring for men, cufflinks if it fits the dress code. For women – subtle earrings (no 1980s power jewels), necklaces, brooches; avoid the distraction that a noisy jangling bracelet will create at interviews.
   o If you haven't updated your glasses for a few years consider investing in a more contemporary style. The right glasses can take years off and the wrong ones add them on!
   o Men should stay away from ties decorated with faces, cartoon characters, numbers, anything that might draw an interviewer's (or customer's) eyes from your face. Choose a tie that complements or brings out your eye colour instead.

You may also want to consider having a full colour, wardrobe and style consultation with an **image consultant**. Prices start from about £80 and most people who have had this done report that it was well worth the time and the money. It made them feel and look more confident and saved them a lot of money in the long run because they stopped buying styles and colours that didn't do anything for them. The two companies mentioned below are the most well known and have many large corporations as clients as well as private individuals. They have local consultants all over the UK.

Many large department stores offer personal shopping services so once you have your rules they can make it even easier for you to keep up to date with each season. It's excellent for busy people, or those who don't really like shopping.

There are tons of women's magazines to help keep up to date with styling; the best place for men is probably *GQ*: the web address is given below.

Essential resources

www.cmb.co.uk Colour me Beautiful offer image and colour consultancy for men and women.

www.houseofcolour.co.uk House of Colour offer image and colour consultancy for men and women.

www.gqmagazine.co.uk *GQ* magazine for men – lots of up-to-date tips on style and grooming. See also **www.gqmagazine.co.uk/Style/How_Often_Should_I/**

Interview insider

Let's imagine now that you have set your sights on your next move, created a winning CV and you're off for that all important interview.

Interviews are a two-way process. The employers have to decide if they want you but you also have to decide if you want them. The odds are usually stacked in favour of the recruiters because they know what they are really looking for irrespective of how well it has been articulated in their ads and job descriptions, and they also get to meet all the other candidates, which usually you don't! So, it's an old cliché but you just have to give it your very best shot. If it's meant to be, it's meant to be. If you don't get the job at least use the interview experience as practice you can learn from and use next time around to give you the edge.

Top tips for interviews

Savvy interviewees will have all their bases covered – this is what the smart plan looks like.

- **Dress:** Select your outfit carefully, taking into account the image tips we've already covered, and take the trouble to find out what the dress code culture is if you want to make a good impression.

- **Travel:** Confirm the date, time and location of the venue, research your travel arrangements and aim to arrive no more than 15 minutes early. Make sure you have a contact phone number just in case you are delayed and need to call them. Keep receipts for your travel - some companies do not offer expenses (those in the public sector usually do) but be prepared to prove how much you spent and offer receipts for reimbursement. Make sure you know or have to hand the name of the person you are meeting so that you can tell reception staff without having to search through your pockets or handbag.

- **Waiting time:** Use your waiting time wisely. You could visit the washrooms and check your appearance, etc., so that when the person who comes to meet you to go to the interview location, you feel relaxed and look your best. You could refresh your memory by referring to your written notes on the ad or the research you have done on the company, the positive things you want to say, etc. Read any in-house magazines you find in the waiting room or reception, as they often give interesting clues about what's going on. Watch how visitors are greeted at reception and the demeanour of employees and visitors as they come and go. It's natural to be a bit nervous but use this time to focus that energy positively.

- **Refreshments:** If you are offered refreshments just opt for water if you are a bit nervous and think balancing a hot cup of tea or coffee might be a distraction. Don't smoke before, during or within view of the interview location even if they invite you to. Never chew gum.

- **First impressions:** Make sure that you make a good first impression on everyone you meet (because you never know what their role might be). Stand up straight, greet with a smile (it shows an accepting attitude towards others) and a firm confident handshake, and make regular eye contact but don't stare and make others feel uncomfortable. You're not there to outshine the person who will be your boss so don't overdo it. If the boss isn't very confident and you are, they might label you as arrogant or feel threatened by you. It won't get you the job. Interviewers will probably engage in pleasantries like 'Hello, pleased to meet you', and ask about your journey and so on – be positive, because they may want to ensure you can get to work regularly on time.

So far, so good. Now at this stage anything could, and often does, happen because of the following variables so it's hard to be prescriptive.

The more senior the job you apply for, the more people you are likely to be interviewed by, and the more likely it is that you may have to take tests or go to an assessment centre where you may have to complete additional tasks, e.g. personality, verbal reasoning, numeracy, role plays and so on. However, these days, most companies take a more team approach to interviewing and it is likely that you will be interviewed by more than one person. Each person will then be required to give their opinion on your suitability and the person with the most votes usually receives the offer. That is of course unless employers decide that no one is suitable, in which case they start all over again (this happens more often than you'd think). If you are applying for a position via a recruitment agency your first interview might be with one of their interviewers because they will probably be paid to filter CVs and candidates. Sometimes the agency will just send you to an interview and you never get to meet a representative, which is really not ideal. You may be lucky, meet the decision maker straight away, only have one interview and receive an offer on the spot. If it's a small firm with little bureaucracy, no time to waste prevaricating or you are the only viable candidate, this could happen.

There are lots of books and courses about how to select and recruit employees but that doesn't necessarily mean that you will meet people who know what they are doing or who follow best practice, even in big companies. Part of the key to good interview practice as a candidate is to expect the unexpected, be prepared to be flexible and appear clam, unruffled and measured in your responses – go with the flow.

I will share with you what I consider to be best or normal practice, however, and that way you can work out what you are being faced with. Believe me, I have met many senior executives who shouldn't be allowed anywhere near a prospective candidate, however, they do so with amazing regularity and no training. Some companies want to see how you perform under pressure and will submit you to seemingly impolite treatment and aggressive questioning; some will take a more relaxed, welcoming stance (and then perhaps go in for the tough questions). Both have their advantages and disadvantages: you can only respond appropriately to what happens in each scenario you encounter. Forewarned, however, is forearmed.

Best practice interviews

- Are held in uncluttered, neutral rooms without interruptions. Bosses who interview on their turf, from behind their chaotic paperwork and keep answering their phone give away a lot about themselves. Is this really a person you could work for? Is this a person who desperately needs help and you're just the person to provide it? Are they just rude and disorganised and likely to treat you badly?
- Have informal seating layouts, or the interviewer will sit adjacent to you rather than opposite you, which can feel confrontational. Panel interviews can be very formal and intentionally intimidating; typically several people face you directly from behind a barrier like a desk while you sit on a chair some distance from the barrier. Always ask where they would like you to sit if they don't indicate a position and then settle down, get your notes out, etc.
- Last no less than an hour, no more than two at a stretch. If you're in there for longer than two hours with a decision maker and it feels relaxed, that is usually a very good sign that they like you. Either that or they have no friends and don't get out much.

- Start with an outline of the interview process. Who *exactly* is going to interview you and what is their role? Roughly how long will you have? The structure – a reprise of the job and the candidate they are looking for, when you will be able to ask questions and so on. You should feel that you understand the process and the route map. Sometimes certain aspects of the job or the way the company operates may have changed; this is their opportunity to let you in on that especially if there has been a longish lead-time between the ad and the first interviews.

- Have a balance of the interviewer talking no more than one third of the time (and preferably only 20%) and the interviewee the remaining time. Good interviewers set the scene, ask questions and *listen*. If they talk the entire time they won't learn anything about you. You need to *listen* too so that you can give a measured response to the question. Take a breath before you reply and maintain eye contact so that you can tell if their eyes start glazing over because you've gone on for too long and they don't know how to shut you up!

- Have a basis for the questions that are asked and a desirable answer. Past performance is not necessarily the most reliable indicator of future performance but it is the most commonly used device in interviews.

  o Sometimes the interviewer will ask you to describe how you might act in a hypothetical situation. The best advice I can give here, if they are not using a method called STAR, is to frame your answer in a STAR manner. STAR stands for Situation, Task, Action, and Result. You recall a situation where something that closely approximates their scenario actually happened, what you then did, what actions you completed and what result ensued (preferably a positive one). This way you reduce the waffle, impress the hell out of them and pick up a few brownie points. Don't claim the glory for something it is obvious you couldn't possibly have achieved, however. This will stand out a mile and reflect badly on your integrity. Sometimes they will refer to this technique as competency based interviewing. It sounds really patronising and often is. Just grin and bear it if you want the job!

o Questions generally revolve around the Big Three mentioned earlier. You have to know how interviewers think in order to satisfy them of your suitability and superiority over other candidates. Think of some practice examples before you go into the interview. You will never have pat answers ready because life isn't like that, but practice will help you to frame thoughtful answers when the time comes.

- **Can you do the job?** This tests skill, experience and track record. Do you have sector experience? Do you have the skill set? International experience? Languages? What could set you apart as well as meet the benchmark? Are you a problem solver or problem maker?

- **Will you do the job?** This tests motivation, commitment and enthusiasm. Will the financial/benefits package keep you in the job for long enough to make it worth the employers' while? Will you go the extra mile? What is your health and attendance track record like?

- **Will you fit in?** This tests your cultural fit with others. Will you complement or disrupt the department? Are you manageable or high maintenance? Will customers warm to you? Can you work alone or in a team? Will you work with others regardless of their gender, race, etc? Can you take direction?

o Question traps that you will lose points on include: failure to listen to the question, annoying the interviewer by answering a question that was not asked, providing superfluous information and waffling, attending the interview having obviously not prepared for it.

o Discriminatory and illegal questions relating to your gender, race, religion, age, family plans and so on should never form part of a professional interview. At this point it is your objective to get a job offer. You can always decline it and make it clear why later.

o Noose questions are those where a negative answer could hang your chances. Typical examples include one I particularly dislike and which usually comes from poor interviewers: 'What is your greatest weakness?' Decline the invitation. Pick up something minor and then immediately show how you deal with it. Turn it into a positive and then wait for the next question.

o Stress questions, the kind that seem aggressive, negative or set you up for a fall – don't take these as personal insults, see them as an opportunity to shine where others will fall. Demonstrate your self-esteem and poise. The interviewer wants to find out what happens to you when the water gets hot – just like real life. If, however, you feel that this is indicative of the way every working day might turn out with that particular boss or company, and it just wouldn't be what you could live with, you can always decide to work elsewhere. That's exactly what they hope you'll do!

o Your questions: should be job related, positive and forward-looking. Don't ask about pay and benefits at this point. Wait until they make you an offer.

One last thing: if you have been made redundant and you get a job interview it probably means that they won't be prejudiced against you as you may have feared. If your former employer's redundancy rationale was public and widely reported in the press they may not even bother to ask you about it. Everyone knows about Lehman Brothers and Woolworths unless they've been living in a cave! If they do ask you they will want a positive answer to explain why you were selected for or opted for redundancy so do practise an acceptable one beforehand. Using this opportunity to vent your spleen about what a useless shower your former boss/colleagues/superiors were won't win you any friends. Admitting you were singled out for the chop because you were an unproductive lump of lard who regularly turned up late, took loads of time off sick and refused to go on any training courses probably won't either. It's all about common sense.

Offers

If all your hard work has paid off, and if you now have multiple offers because you have been chasing several opportunities at once, then – good for you! You are in a great position now. You have more information at your disposal so make sure that you don't lose your head at this stage and just accept the first offer. Get the best overall package you can, and make sure that it matches all the criteria that you set out for yourself in Chapter 5.

Essential resources

If you buy only one book on this topic make it *Great Answers to Tough Interview Questions*, by Martin John Yate, Kogan Page ISBN 0-7494-4356-1.

Chapter 7 Starting work again – survival tactics

In the relief and euphoria that you experience once you are back on a payroll, you may not be prepared for the shock of entering a new organisation, especially if you don't have much previous experience of job change. You will be going through a period of change again so please recognise the bumps in that process I mentioned in Chapter 3. They're normal.

Dealing with change effectively is a bit like having a vaccination and building up anti-bodies to ward off the negative effects in order to cope more easily, more quickly the next time something happens. The first time you experience something new or different it's easy to feel uncomfortable and hesitant but gradually you create ways of surviving, evolving and coming through the other side. Besides, you haven't really lived if you don't have a few scars! What counts is how you deal with them after all.

So, once you have an acceptable offer and a start date, ask your employers what kind of induction programme there will be for you so that you can get up the learning curve quickly and start making a real contribution. Put that way it will appear positive and even if they hadn't thought of organising anything it could be just the prompt they need. Even better, if they look askance at such a suggestion, give them an indication of what you might need and why it will help – access to the intranet, passwords, procedural familiarisation, background reports to whatever is relevant, not just the normal toilets-and-tea-machine routine most people are subjected to.

The best companies I have worked with recognise that an effective induction programme is essential to retaining new employees. A good induction programme will not overwhelm you on the first day. Your employers ought to: make sure you have a base or home straight away; not subject you to endless death-by-PowerPoint presentations; assign a buddy to watch out for you; only introduce you to a few key people at a time; assign you the tools to do the job quickly and give you something real to do as soon as possible.

As a consultant who helps organisations solve their business problems, I am usually called in where there is trouble brewing so I may have a more cynical view of induction failure than most. Induction is, however, a sadly neglected area and leads to the shocking statistics of high turnover for new employees at all levels of the organisation. In the Chartered Institute of Personal Development (CIPD) *Recruitment, Retention and Turnover Report 2004*, the focus group was struck by the high proportion of early departures among new staff; one in five new employees leave after less than six months, and half the leaving population have only two years' service. This is a waste of the employers' money and potentially damaging for the employee too and it doesn't seem to have improved much over the years.

Top tips for your first day

- Be as prepared as possible and remember that first impressions count.
- Be nice to everyone you meet because you will have no idea how pleasant or unpleasant they could make your life later on – especially porters, security guards, secretaries, canteen staff, the person who looks after the stationery cupboard, etc.

- Don't just make a beeline for the great and the powerful and get a reputation as an untrustworthy, party line suck-up from the start. Mix with your peers and co-workers too.
- Be and look busy.
- Be prepared to put in a few extra hours to get used to things in the early days.
- Take papers home to read or mug up on key information during your daily commute, if you have one.
- Learn as much about the company culture as possible so that you can work with it rather than clash head on.
- Unless there are fundamental, show stopping gaps between what they told you at your interview and the reality of your job (like being paid half what they offered you), it's best to just plough through it. Nothing ever really works out that neatly.
- Remember work places can be a bit like playgrounds, so watch out for the bullies, try not to get involved in gangs and don't let anyone steal your lunch money!

A slight amount of rose-tinting often goes on at interviews. However, I owe many of my best opportunities to discovering work that was never part of my official job or discussed at an interview. I've also had my fair share of corporate manure to shovel as well. In real life we have to find our own silver linings.

Essential resources

The Rules of Work, Richard Templar, Prentice Hall Business ISBN 0-273-66271-6

Power: The 48 Laws, Robert Greene & Joost Elffers, Profile Books Ltd ISBN 1-86197 488-4

Think and Grow Rich, Napoleon Hill, The Wilshire Book Company ISBN 0-87980-163-8

Chapter 8 Running your own business

After going through the trials of redundancy one or more times it can seem awfully tempting to start your own business, especially if you're lucky enough to be given a lump sum settlement.

A report from small business insurer More Than Business found that there is a growing trend of what are being dubbed 'alterpreneurs'. These are people who quit corporate life to start their own business as a lifestyle rather than a career choice: 60% of those surveyed said they wanted to get more control over their lives, and 54% said they made their entrepreneurial move in order to be 'happier'. They make up nearly 70% of the UK's small business market, running approximately 2 million micro-businesses and generating over £2 billion in annual revenue.

Whatever you decide is, of course, up to you but here are some pointers that you'll probably find useful.

Making sure you survive

Business survival through the first three years is critical so plan for success right from the beginning is vital particularly in the current economic climate. This includes: all of the financial and legal aspects (cash flow management being the key critical area) as well as defining products and services that customers want, need or are willing to pay for in sufficient numbers.

According to Michael Ames in his book *Small Business Management* and *Gustave Berle's *The Do It Yourself Business Book* **the main reasons for business failure** are:

- lack of experience
- insufficient capital
- poor location
- poor inventory management
- over-investment in fixed assets
- poor credit arrangements
- personal use of business funds
- unexpected growth
- competition*
- low sales*

The message is clear – do your homework, put together a decent business plan and enter the marketplace hopefully but prudently. Plenty of doomsayers like to put people off taking risks. The Brits, unlike the Americans, have a more cautious approach to new ventures but as long as you have the passion, the drive to go for your goals and both seek and use the plentiful advice out there to make a success of your venture then I say – go for it!

Raising capital

The capital used to start and run a business typically comes from a variety of sources: savings, gifts or private loans (from family and friends), redundancy settlements, sale of assets (houses, etc.), bank loans and overdrafts, grants and venture capital.

In addition, there are more informal sources of investment, such as 'business angels'. Business angels are an alternative to venture capital providers, as a source of smaller amounts of equity capital. These investors are private individuals, usually with a business background. They are willing to make investments in small businesses in return for an equity stake. They can also offer the benefits of their own management expertise.

For more information contact **www.businesslink.gov.uk** or the National Business Angels Network on 020 7329 2929.

Programmes such as the BBC's *Dragon's Den* have done much to raise the profile of

this type of financing but if you've watched any of these episodes, where unprepared entrepreneurs are literally thrown to the dragons, you'll understand how valuable it is to be on the ball and know your numbers, trademark and patent protections, and have a scalable, sustainable business proposition.

Some other financing resources you may find useful.

www.primeinitiative.org.uk specialises in finance for businesses for the over 50s.

www.clearlybusiness.com Barclays Bank small/new business support arm.

Business types

When it comes to deciding which route to follow, there are **three main areas** to consider.

- setting up a business from scratch using your own idea
- buying an existing business to run

- buying a franchise – the rights to an existing business formula and branding

There are plenty of information sites to investigate each of these three options – these are listed in the Essential resources section later on there is a more comprehensive section on the New Life website. Do remember, however, to consult the services of an experienced accountant or legal professional before you buy a business or to check out your business plan.

Starting your own business, particularly if you haven't any previous experience, can be a risky endeavour. The benefit of option 3, **franchising**, is that you buy into an off-the-shelf business model – the branding, processes, standards, product sourcing and so on are already created for you, and training is usually part of the package. Actually, if no training is offered that could be your signal to back off, but you also need to make sure that you are getting value for money. Learning to run the business operationally is one thing but what you also need is advice and support on selling to your customers successfully. Buying into a franchise doesn't preclude you from using any of the other business support services that are offered by Business Link or the high street banks, so make sure you get all the advice and help you can.

Even with all the pre-packaging there is still a lot of work to be done to run a successful franchise and it means a lot of hard graft, especially at the beginning.

Franchises vary in terms of their level of required investment and track record, so do shop around before you commit yourself. Your choice should reflect the lifestyle you want to build as well as create an attractive income stream. At the risk of repeating myself, although I will, because it is so important, you must consult the services of an experienced accountant or legal professional before you buy into a franchise and most banks have experienced advisors on this topic, as they are very often the ones lending the money to buy into them. Don't forget that as well as your stake money you will be required to find your working capital and also be able to survive financially until your business yields adequate returns.

I've got an idea – now what?

To start a business in a sector in which you are already working is really the best way forward. You understand it, you know where to get your supplies and you have experience of the market. But if your idea involves stepping into pastures new, focus on research and finding your niche.

Step 1: create your business plan

What are you going to sell? Who are you going to sell to? What kind of experience are you going to create for your customers? What's the competition and how are you going to be better than them? How are you going to reach your customers? When are you planning to start? Who will work in your business? What will your brand stand for? Where will you operate your business from? How much are you hoping to sell over what period? What forms of distribution will you use: internet, retail, door to door, mail order, etc?

Most of the banks and Business Link have sample business plan templates you can use. Use these to help you with financing as they will be geared to that decision-making model and you won't have to do the work twice over. Again, you'll find more free downloads, templates and information resources at www.newlifenetwork.co.uk.

Step 2: work out all your financials fully

What start-up capital will you need? The bigger your start up capital, the more you need to sell to recoup it, so how can you save money? What does your cash flow forecast look like? What will your break-even point be and how long might it take to achieve it? How much working capital will you need and for how long? Will it cover your payroll costs, materials or stock costs? What will your pricing strategy be? How big a marketing budget will you need? These are all fundamentally important issues that will form part of your business plan and ongoing management strategy. Who will manage your finances? If you don't have someone the banks trust in charge, it is unlikely that they will lend you money particularly in the current climate.

Step 3: find premises to operate from

Unless you're going into retail you may be able to use a serviced office, incubator premises or temporary address to start off with. Your local Business Link advisors should be able to help with this. Never do work to a building until you have had it surveyed and signed the lease or freehold documentation.

Step 4: sort out the legalities

- What is the best model for your business? Sole trader, partnership, limited company? Each model has its advantages and disadvantages. Seek advice from your accountant and they will help you with the most appropriate model and set it up for you for a reasonable fee.
- Should you register for value added tax (VAT)? If your taxable supplies, distance   sales, or acquisitions are expected to exceed £67,000 in the next 30 days, or if you are already trading, and they have exceeded £67,000 in

the past 12 months or, if you have taken over a VAT registered business as a going concern, then you must notify your Customs and Excise local VAT office immediately of your liability to register for VAT. If not, you can register voluntarily. Most items carry the standard prevailing rate but there are exceptions and it pays to know what they are. This means you can reclaim the VAT you pay out but you must levy it on what you sell. This pushes up prices on low turnover consumer trading but has many advantages if you only deal with businesses. You can register on a cash basis so that you only pay the VAT to the authorities when your customers pay you. Find out more here: **www.hmrc.gov.uk**

- What do you need to tell the Inland Revenue? Plenty! Find out more here: **www.hmrc.gov.uk**
- Do you need to secure trade marks or patents to protect your business ideas and names? Find out more here: **www.patent.gov.uk**
- Will you need to register under the data protection laws? Find out more here: **www.informationcommissioner.gov.uk**
- What type of contracts or insurance might you need? Business Link is a good source of information on this area.

Step 5: Sort out the practicalities

Will you need business cards, stationery, staff, telephones, computers, etc? It can take a while to find the best places to secure your supplies and people but wise investments in equipment and staff will pay huge dividends so it is important not to skimp on this stage.

Step 6: Get going!

Customers do not buy from businesses if they don't know that they exist. What will your marketing strategy be? Where and how will you sell your products and services? How can you get free publicity through the press or word of mouth via customers or key contacts? How will you use networking PR to promote your business? Check out Paula Gardner's excellent site **www.doyourownpr.com**

Remember it could take much longer to pull all the strands together than you think so don't hang about once you've set your mind on your goals.

Essential resources

www.businesslink.gov.uk National government network to support commerce. Each regional site has its own specialities, priorities and energy level. They are the best place to go first if you are at all confused about the patchwork of development agencies and business development quangos there are around.

www.taforum.org The Trade Association Forum, established in 1997. Housed along with the Confederation of British Industry (CBI).

Their website contains a search facility for all the different trade associations in the UK.

www.britishchambers.org.uk British Chambers of Commerce.

www.startinbusiness.co.uk Information-rich site on everything you need to research before making a decision to buy an existing business, a franchise, becoming an agent or re-seller or starting from scratch.

www.startups.co.uk Solid information site for start-ups.

http://thetraderonline.com created by Richard Grady whose ebook *The UK-Trader's UK Wholesale Guide* has become a best seller. Excellent for budding e-commerce traders and eBay fans.

www.smallbusiness.co.uk Help and tips especially for small businesses.

www.daltonsbusiness.com A lively site for looking at businesses for sale.

www.british-franchise.org This should be your first stop when researching franchising. Independent, in that it carries no franchising ads but it is sponsored by all the UK retail banks.

www.franinfo.co.uk Lots of information about franchising.

http://uk.betheboss.com Comprehensive franchise information site.

Chapter 9 Getting a trade

These days, lots of people swap a corporate job for a good old-fashioned trade or set up a business inspired by their hobby or home-based skills. You may want to set up on your own or work for another company as a plumber, carpenter, plasterer, lorry driver, gardener, gas boiler engineer, handyman (or woman), interior designer, alternative therapist or set up a cleaning or ironing business. To do this you may need to re-train, and there are some places listed later on to help you get started – you'll find the most current list at www.newlifenetwork.co.uk. You may also need to set up your own business entity.

For most of the trades listed you should consult an accountant or Business Link consultant to advise you on the best structure to adopt. If there are commercial risks, it makes good sense to use a limited-liability company or partnership. This can protect you personally from risks, such as being sued by a customer or being exposed to claims from suppliers. Sometimes the companies you work for will insist on dealing with you as a limited company. The administrative burden is greater than that of sole trader and the accounts are on public record, filed at Companies House, but a good accountant will help you set up appropriate recording systems that are not too onerous or expensive.

Some of the ideas in the Get wired section later on will help you sort out what you will need to run your business. In addition, you may need to invest in some basic business cards, the tools of your trade, a van or other suitable form of transport, a home office or consulting room, a simple website or an entry in Yellow Pages or similar. Word of mouth referrals are generally the best form of marketing in these types of businesses and don't underestimate the power of your local Parish magazine.

It may take a while for business to flow in but many report more work flowing in than they can cope with once they are established, if they are providing a value-for-money, reliable service in their local community.

Some training providers will try to tell you that you can learn all you need to know on an online course or via distance learning packages. While these methods have a useful role to play you absolutely have to have hands-on practice and guidance from experienced people to be any good at all. Best avoid the get rich quick offers, I think!

Essential resources

Training providers and resources

Public training courses

www.hotcourses.com The leading place to find any course in the UK; has the UK's largest and most accurate database of educational opportunities.

Lorry driving

www.careersinlogistics.co.uk A very comprehensive site, covering training schools, earnings, legal stuff, etc. There is a huge shortage of HGV drivers so plenty of opportunities there.

Plumbing

www.iphe.org.uk The Institute of Plumbing and Heating Engineers gives you pretty much all you need to know. Many Further Education courses are oversubscribed and more and more private providers are springing up.

www.plumbinfo.co.uk provides some interesting background on training.

Gas installation

www.britishgasacademy.co.uk The British Gas Academy

www.sbgi.org.uk The Society of British Gas Engineers

Carpentry

www.central-office.co.uk/ioc Institute of Carpenters

Interior design

www.bida.org The British Interior Design Association. The Association does not maintain a list of courses available or offer a formal careers advisory service; however, it acts as a portal to just about everywhere else that does.

Landscape gardening

www.lantra.co.uk/Landscaping The Sector Skills Council for the environmental and land based sector. Landscaping covers the design, planning, creation and maintenance of designed landscapes, both urban and rural, and the interiors of buildings.

It involves everything from the management of sports turf, golf courses, parks and historic gardens to planning domestic gardens and leisure facilities. Estimates say the landscape industry is made up of nearly 38,000 businesses employing approximately 112,000 people. These people will be employed in a range of different-sized organisations, from local authority departments, parks and gardens, to domestic and commercial landscape companies, to self-employed landscape contractors. There are different sectors of the industry, ranging from those that work on large construction projects, like motorway maintenance, to services for people and companies such as landscape gardening.

Franchises

Franchises to set up as driving instructors, locksmiths, estate agents and so on are all worth exploring. See Chapter 8 on running your own business and franchising.

Teaching

A profession as opposed to a trade, I know. Over a third of new teaching recruits are over 30. It's not a soft option by any means but this country needs a lot of good quality, passionate teachers so why not check out your options at **www.teachernet.gov.uk**, **www.prospects.ac.uk**,**www.tda.gov.uk**, **www.teachinginscotland.co.uk**.

Primary teaching places are oversubscribed but secondary schools are desperate for teachers with degrees in languages, science, maths, design and technology and there are grants and incentives for those areas.

If you don't fancy teaching school children you could consider **adult learning**. If you're good at any kind of **building trade** it's estimated that more than half of the current lecturers and trainers in this area will retire over the next five years leaving courses with nobody to teach them. Could you take their places? Contact your local Further Education College to find out what opportunities they might have. Alternatively, you could enrol on a part-time teaching course so that you can be ready and waiting when the vacancies occur.

Alternative therapies

www.itecworld.co.uk The Reflexology International Therapy Examination Council. Also see your local FE College, as they are usually the main providers for beauty therapy training

Image consultants

www.cmb.co.uk Colour Me Beautiful

www.tfic.org.uk The Federation of Image Consultants

Chapter 10 Becoming a consultant or freelancer

When redundancy has suddenly curtailed a career you enjoyed and trained and worked hard for a very common option for business professionals is to become a consultant in, for example, IT, HR, project management, marketing, PR or management consultancy. Many of the most interesting boutique practices have begun because talented individuals have broken away from bigger firms or been made redundant when billings have looked dangerously low.

Three things are really important whatever route you take.

1 You do need to be **really good** at something, i.e. have real expertise in an industry or a business discipline, or you won't get any initial clients, repeat business or referrals. You need to be able to apply that expertise and knowledge in a setting other than your old company.

2 You have to be **good at selling and marketing** – selling yourself, selling your ideas, selling your prices, selling your methodologies. You may be good at what you do but how are you going to get the work? Selling in this context is hard for newcomers especially if you have either no experience or you have only sold to a captive internal audience in your previous role. You have to have the courage to ask for the order, learn how to close and be comfortable networking and looking for business. If you have no idea what I'm talking about, get yourself on a course so you do, because you won't survive otherwise.

3 You have to be good at **building relationships** with clients and understand your accountability to them or you won't get any business the first time or any time after that.

How do I start?

You can go via the **interim management** route (see Chapter 11).

You can become a **portfolio worker,** where you work for a variety of companies concurrently. This means you have several income streams, and client organisations still get access to expertise that perhaps they don't need or can't afford to employ on a full-time basis or beyond a specific event.

Or, you can become a **freelance contractor.** This has been a very popular route, especially for IT professionals. Essentially you work for (usually) one client or project at a time for the contract duration. You must be very careful of the Inland Revenue implications of IR35. The best place to go for all kinds of advice and services in this area is:

The Professional Contractors Group Ltd
Heathrow Boulevard
280 Bath Road
West Drayton
UB7 0DQ
Tel: 0845 125 9899
Website: www.pcg.org.uk

Freelancers often work as **associates** of other organisations. You may be self-employed but wear the hat, so to speak, of the organisation you represent. Trainers and management consultants often register for work with several organisations as part of an informal network or bank of approved providers. For trainers and coaches a good resource is Trainer Base at **www.trainerbase.co.uk**. CIPD or ITOL membership for trainers is almost obligatory, it seems.

The best place to start researching for information and training in management or business is relatively recently formed Institute of Business Consulting at **www.ibconsulting.org.uk**.

These days everyone seems to be obsessed with **qualifications** – how many, where from, are they dumbed down from 'my day'? It can work against the over-40s who have lots of experience and have undergone company training which has not been recognised by some authorising body that might not even have existed (or at least in the same form) when you started out. We all know that qualification or certification is no real guarantee that a person can do a decent job (and building up a publishable set of referrals from former clients is essential) but nevertheless you will need to start building up a series of signals which point to you being worth employing. If you are reading this before you need to leave your current job, you should consider looking at the Chartered Manager scheme with the CMI at **www.managers.org**.

When marketing yourself then (which includes what you put on your business card), having a degree, an MBA, a post-graduate qualification or sporting the appropriate letters of a **trade association** that you are a member of is vital. You have to be very careful which ones you register with unless you have very deep pockets but most do offer more than just a certificate. The Chartered Institute of Management (which also incorporates The Institute of Business Consulting at www.ibconsulting.org.uk) is reasonable value for money. What you really want to evaluate each fee against is: whether or not it gives you access to industry news, so you can keep up to date; what networking opportunities it offers; and somewhere to market your CV or company services. If the organisation throws in a magazine and a reasonably priced conference, so much the better. Another common sense marketing advice site worth looking at is **www.clientmagnet.com** run by Bernadette Doyle or Paula Gardner's excellent **www.doyourownpr.com**.

What should I invest in?

To set up, you will need as modest or as de-luxe a set of resources you want to fund depending on your chosen route. It may look something like the following list (look at the Get wired section later on too) and run to a few thousand pounds depending on whether you are starting from scratch or not.

- A laptop, carrying case, printer (maybe fax or scanner if necessary).
- Appropriate business software – Microsoft Office or similar, anti-virus software, adware protection and a firewall or buy an iMac, far more reliable I find.
- An internet account, preferably unlimited broadband.
- An email address (preferably not Hotmail).
- A website – a cheap but well executed DIY job or something fancier if you must.
- An appropriate vehicle for travelling to and from clients, etc.
- A home office space with a decent, back-supporting chair and filing space.
- LCD projector, portable screen, flip chart and pens (only if you really need to provide this yourself).

- An office address but not necessarily real space (it could be your accountant's address).
- Business stationery – cards (your most important asset), a basic letterhead.
- A simple logo/business identity – DIY or through an inexpensive local designer.
- Basic office supplies – folders, plastic wallets, Post-Its, pens, stamps, etc.
- An appointment system – paper or electronic diary.
- A mobile and a landline with an answering machine facility.
- Professional Indemnity Insurance (usually at a discount through your Trade Association).
- A membership budget for networking and Trade Associations.
- A marketing budget for any activities you deem necessary (try and blag as much free stuff as possible and use any free PR avenues you can).
- A core compendium of documents to market yourself: mini presentation, CV.
- A core compendium of documents/spreadsheets to manage expenses, invoices. You probably don't need anything as fancy as SAGE. Excel will do if you send out a few high value invoices per month and have limited expenses.
- An allowance for your accounts, VAT returns, company registration, etc., to be completed.
- An allowance for re-training and skill development.
- An allowance to live on while you are waiting for your invoices to be paid (be very, very good at sending out and getting invoices paid!)

You may need to register with the **Data Protection Registrar**, for **VAT**, as a **limited company** and so on but take advice from your accountant and look at the Business Link sites for more specific advice.

You should always **start small** and build up on the expense side. Use serviced offices if you need to, rent or lease whatever you need instead of buying so as to make your money go further. Have meetings in nice coffee shops and get to know the better hotel lounges in your area. Many of my friends who are members of the Institute of Directors use their meeting rooms on Pall Mall when they are in London meeting with other consultants and some clients. It has a nice dining room too.

As far as **fees** go there are averages for each industry type. Go to your particular Trade Association for advice on freelance rates both regionally and for London (usually a vast difference) and be careful how much free stuff you do for clients. More than 66,000 businesses in the UK are registered with management consultancy as a core activity so there are a lot of players out there but don't be tempted to subsidise them if you can't afford it or if they don't buy from you in a reasonable manner. You should always consider your down time when deciding on your fees, build in holiday, admin days, selling days, etc. A really good independent can earn £50K per annum or more which isn't a bad living, but it's not a route paved with gold and Porsches despite what the media would have you believe.

Make sure you have ways of **keeping up to date** – it's easy to get out of touch when you aren't part of a big company any more. The internet is fantastic for this and lots of places will deliver free newsletters to your electronic mail box. I like **www.silicon.com** for the IT updates, **www.personneltoday.com** for the HR updates, Harvard Business Review Working Knowledge site **http://hbswk.hbs.edu** for cutting edge management thinking, the CMI **www.managers.org.uk** for more home-grown issues; or subscribe to **www.timesonline.co.uk** business bulletins.

Get wired

You may have access to a computer at work or a library but I can't stress enough how important it is for people of all ages to both get computer savvy and have their own computers to use at home. Being able to word process documents, create presentations, spreadsheets, use the internet to search for jobs, information and advice, learn online and even set up and run a website for your business or interest is so vital and really easy to do. Get friends, your kids, your local FE College and so on to help you get wired and steer you in the right direction. Have a look in the training section in this book or on www.newlifenetwork.co.uk for other places to learn.

If you want to set up a **home office** or you're thinking of setting up as any kind of consultant or web entrepreneur you'll need a workspace and equipment to help you.

The basics

- A desk, storage cabinet and a back–supporting computer chair in a place with good natural light, preferably in a spot where no one else will disturb your thoughts or paperwork.

- You can build a website quickly and cheaply at hosting sites like **www.1and1internet.com** without the need for programming skills. See Chapter 12 for more information.

- A computer with as much memory as you can afford with the most up-to-date operating system, Windows Vista, XP or Mac compatible. Make sure you have all the proper anti-virus software, a firewall and adware protection (possibly more irksome than virus infection these days). If you need to go and visit clients or work on their site then get a laptop, as light as possible with a good quality carrying case. Shop around and see what you like before you buy because it's a very important investment.

- Some people are definitely Mac fans rather than PC fans. Either will do the job though, having become an iMac user, I personally wouldn't ever want to use anything else.

- Get a reasonably heavy-duty printer – I have a small colour printer/scanner and a separate black and white workhorse printer.
- If you have a digital camera, it can be handy for uploading images to your website or into presentations. Quite cheap cameras with high pixel counts are now readily available.
- Use broadband if you can get it. It is relatively inexpensive now and essential for speedy work on the internet. BT, AOL etc. all have packages of varying speed and price. If you live in a poorly-cabled area like me don't pay for the higher value packages if BT can't pipe it in.
- A telephone with an answering machine (and a polite and friendly recorded message), and a basic mobile phone so customers can reach you wherever you are, are a must.
- Some basic stationery and office supplies are also essential. Order online and have them delivered directly to your home address to avoid lugging heavy boxes around. Many online companies have next day delivery services.

Chapter 11 Interim management

Post redundancy you might find that **interim management** is suggested to you as a new career option. There has been rather a lot of hype, spin and lack of reliable data about this growing market so I'll try my best to make things clearer. According to my sources, around 200-plus companies claim to be providers, many are recruitment firms jumping on the bandwagon and some are simply re-branding 'contracting' as 'interim'. The market is reckoned to be worth £500 million and there are around 8,000 interims operating today.

Employers and agencies alike consider interim personnel as part of the flexible resourcing options that are common in today's job market, with more and more interim workers being under the age of 45. The **public sector** are big users of interims (not always at a particularly senior level) and private sector managers with the right skill set who can cope with the significant cultural differences could find it an interesting challenge. It's a courageous but potentially very rewarding career choice.

Interims are not contractors or consultants. The term interim management refers to the rapid provision of senior executives to manage change or transition.

Interim managers are commissioned on an assignment basis and act as senior managers for a third party. They should be free to focus specifically on the assignment in hand, available immediately and leave when no longer required. Unlike consultants they take line responsibility, implement, share in confidential decision-making, are sensibly over-qualified, and are fully accountable to the client. **The Institute of Interim Management** assert that interim management is defined by three interlocking characteristics:

- the seniority of the temporary role being filled
- the quality of briefing, selection and screening processes used to find suitable candidates
- the support service provided from placement to completion of the assignment.

In addition, they say that interim managers ought to have a proven track record of achievement and of adding tangible value to the bottom line of the organisation. They should be used to delivering on time and to budget, be experienced problem solvers, strategic thinkers and accustomed to rolling up their sleeves and actually doing the job. I'm pretty sure too that the ability to build productive relationships and do so quickly, along with strong influencing skills, would also be high on the list of a truly successful interim.

It's amazing really that the ranks of such super-managers are often swelled by previously redundant executives. It makes you wonder why their former employers didn't hang on to them or whether they had ever enabled them to deploy their skills properly in the first place, doesn't it?

Benefits

The pros of employing interim managers for employers are that they can give the tough jobs to people who may be able to stand the heat given that they will be able to see the light at the end of the tunnel and leave when the job is done. It is definitely an 'on/off' tap or a 'try before you buy' option for them (should the position become a permanent one) without the pain and expense of re-deploying someone once the party's over.

For interims, it can be a way of finding a stream of challenges, if that is what motivates them, a way of adding something valuable to their CV, a method of acquiring experience not previously available to them, a way of simply staying employed or of creating a niche that may perhaps lead to a full-time job offer.

An old friend of mine has been doing it for years, I spotted her photo featured in a Daily Telegraph article on the topic as an increasingly attractive career option for **women** who want more control over their work patterns or see it as an opportunity to gain additional skills and experience. Russams now operate a networking group for women interims that is well worth checking out.

Fees

Fees vary enormously from £500 to £1500 per day (though Russams research suggest that they average around £550) so the rewards can be high but there will be a reason why the fees are high. It will pay to check what the assignment demands to justify such a fee and of course there aren't the benefit packages, such as pensions and so on, that you might be used to receiving as a full-time employee. You must be self-employed, set up a limited company and have professional indemnity insurance.

Risk management

Some say that interim management can fit well with portfolio working, but interims tend to be employed pretty much full-on, whereas portfolio workers tend to spread their risk and have their eggs in several baskets at the same time. Having done both, I can say that it is hard to juggle both approaches successfully. If an interim role is part-time, however, it does make a useful addition to a portfolio. A long gap between assignments can make it hard to slot back into portfolio or freelance working again but on the positive side it could fund a few nice long holidays or a chance to indulge a hobby in between each one. Others report that long interim assignments can mean that carefully cultivated networks for consultancy can easily wither so be careful that you have a proactive re-entry strategy for another interim job, post-assignment.

Where do assignments come from?

There are three key areas:

- Gap management: cover for maternity leavers, illness and sudden departures.
- Project management: introducing new systems, moves, new market developments, outsourcing.
- Corporate change management: start-ups, flotations, turnarounds, etc.

Most importantly two out of every three engagements are won by interims themselves by direct contact with clients, so networking is all-important.

Training

The Interim Management Association (IMA) offers a one-day workshop through Results in Business (www.results-in-business.com) that could be paid for by employers as part of an outplacement package (about £395 + VAT) or at a discount for individuals (about £339 + VAT).

This is the only official workshop accredited by the UK Interim Management Association, designed specifically for executives and managers considering interim management as a career choice. It is also accredited and supported by the Institute of Interim Managers. You can book a place and check live availability at www.ima-institute.com.

The workshop aims to provide an objective and independent service for delegates, enabling them to make an informed decision on whether interim management is right for them and, if so, how to go about making it a reality in the shortest time and most effective way.

It includes benchmarking skills against the industry standard and expectations, examining the core competencies highly regarded in top candidates and, critically, the route to engagement with leading accredited service providers. It also covers information on how to set up in business, including appropriate legislation, and the risks and potential rewards of self-employment in the interim world. A certificate of completion is awarded post-workshop for you to include with your application to service providers.

Placement

If you do go down this road, before you start an interim contract, be sure to agree a thorough brief in writing. This should include:

- as tight a set of achievement goals and objectives as possible
- clearly understood parameters of authority, resources and accountability
- firm arrangements about start and completion dates
- a high-impact induction programme so that you can hit the ground running as soon as possible
- payment schedules, early completion bonuses, etc.

If the prospective employer can't furnish you with any of these vital elements, keep at it until they do because the risk of not doing so can be significant for both parties. This is how many jobs go pear-shaped for people, whatever they are labelled. So, you really do have to be firm, however much you want to start earning and achieving.

Essential resources

www.interimmanagement.uk.com The Interim Management Association also has a list of recruitment agencies specialising in interim placements. The IMA is the **industry trade body** representing the supply companies such as Global Executives and Ashton Penney.

www.ioim.org.uk The Institute of Interim Managers. The IIM is the **institute** that represents executives who practise as interim managers. A good source of information on trends and best practice, recruiters and partners. The establishment of the Institute of Interim Management marked an important milestone in the development of Interim management as a recognised professional discipline. In affiliation with the industry trade body, the Interim Management Association (IMA, formerly ATIES) and the Chartered Management Institute (CMI), the IIM was launched in April 2001.

www.globalexecutives.com Interim recruitment

www.ashtonpenney.com Interim recruitment

www.russam-gms.co.uk Interim manager recruitment and industry researchers

Chapter 12 Web entrepreneur

The internet has brought us mixed blessings. Along with rather dubious adult content sites and the perfect way for the ill-intentioned to rob or terrorise us, it has provided us with ways of finding information and buying goods and services that were previously unimaginable. Once the initial silliness of the dot.com bubble burst, plenty of companies created a powerful presence on the net as their sole channel of distribution or as a useful additional channel.

So, if you want to try making your new life as a web entrepreneur, what do you need to know? Once again, there are a trillion books out there but this is a fast-moving area, so here are the highlights, and then it's up to you to work out your own individual solutions.

The first point I want to make is that all the other normal rules of business still apply. You still need a decent business plan, vision, financials, etc. Having a business in cyberspace does not exempt you from thinking things through properly or obeying the law and complying with the tax authorities.

As I walk down my local high street I see shops and eateries that are shining examples of their genre and have been in business for ever, and I also see plenty of shoddy or badly staffed 'Johnny-come-latelys' that may or may not make a buck before they either adapt, survive and become better or go under. The internet is just the same only it just isn't so obvious. A badly organised site with poor navigation can be as bad as a shop that is merchandised like a jumble sale. A slow and unresponsive site can have the same effect on your shopping experience as a long queue at the Post Office or a surly shop assistant. You may never buy there again, you may not buy from there at all and what's more you'll tell everyone you know not to shop there either! Would you shop somewhere where they can't give you a receipt, or pay in advance if you think they might rip you off? No – which is why you need proper security measures on sites that accept credit transactions. OK, I'm sure you get the picture. However, when you build your site you must incorporate these things into your thinking.

What you do and how you do it are then really functions of: your familiarity with the internet, the time you have to create a DIY site or farm it out to a professional, your budget, the level of sophistication you really need, and so on.

Web essentials

Domain names

Every site needs to have its own a domain name – this is the **www.whatyoursiteiscalled.com** (or co.uk or .co.org or .co.biz or .co.net, etc., etc.). That is how your sign is found on the World Wide Web (the internet) when customers type your address into the search engine (Google, Yahoo, etc.) to find your site. It's just an address. The best address is a dot.com, followed by dot.co.uk or whatever country you need to use (de = Germany for instance – think car licence plates). dot.org tends to be for government or official public sites, dot.ac for education (or academic). Obviously you can't have the same address as anyone else so you must register your unique address and pay a fee to do so and prove that you own it. Loads of companies on the net offer to do this for you very cheaply. It depends on how you build your site, though, so read on. Short, snappy, easily remembered addresses are best, not least because they are less prone to typing errors. You then need to register them with the search engines either manually or by using special software programmes. It's like deciding your address and then telling the cyber equivalent of the Royal Mail where to find you. It's that simple.

Design

Essentially, you have three options:

1. Hire a professional who is a freelancer or part of a web design company.
2. Learn how to programme and do it yourself using popular software packages e.g. Adobe Dreamweaver.
3. Do it -yourself using a simple hosting package that requires no programming skills.

So, how to choose?

If all you want is a simple three-page site with limited functionality to advertise your freelance consulting business, your plumbing business, your new restaurant, etc., then I'd probably go for **option three**. There are some downsides but they are so minimal it's hardly worth thinking about. There are other providers so choose what you feel most comfortable with after a little research, but if you use a provider like www.doyourownsite.co.uk you can put up and maintain a perfectly adequate site for anywhere between £8 to £15 per month. Because they have huge economies of scale they can offer you lots of bells and whistles for very low prices.

You choose a template from their selection and create what you like as though you were typing a Word document. Also, for very low sums you can often organise your web and email addresses with them, and host your site (a bit like permanent car parking for your site kept on their computer servers). You can add weblogs (online diaries), voting forums, chat rooms, picture galleries, e-shops, newsletters, graphics, links, etc. Some also give you free software to register your site with the major search engines, Photoshop software and so on. You can go on and amend your site whenever you like, so it is very flexible.

It's worth setting one up to play with and get used to it so that when you want something more flash, you are capable of giving the designers a decent brief. It's almost like live field research. You can find out what works and what doesn't before you pay out more money.

Going on a course and **designing it yourself.** You will probably find courses at your local Further Education college, which will give you a huge advantage if you like that kind of thing. You have to consider how long a course will take and cost and how much time you have to do that as opposed to all the other things you will need to do to set your business up.

The other alternative is to **get someone else to do it.**

- Your local Business Link contact will probably know who's who in the area. You can go on to one of their supplier databases or find one on the internet.
- If you can't do this, or you don't like their site or examples of the work they have done for other customers, then don't use them. You can spend thousands of pounds on this option and if you really need sophisticated tools, lots of storage, etc., then go ahead – but pick someone you respect and for goodness' sake give them a decent written brief.
- If you've already created a DIY site use that to show them what you want and what else you need.
- They need to know what you are going to use your site for; whether you have any graphics or if they need to research them for you or take photographs; whether you

have payment mechanisms set up already or not; and what levels of traffic you expect.

- Don't let them start until you have agreed on the written brief and a project schedule and a price.
- Prices should include the one-off design and any subsequent alterations, page additions or copy changes. If you keep changing your mind, they will quite rightly keep charging you more and take longer!

Design notes

- Don't go for every bell and whistle and piece of flash animation or high-density graphics just because you or the designer can do it.
- You want the pages to download as quickly as possible or your visitors will go elsewhere. If it doesn't add value, don't do it.
- Stick to limited numbers of fonts, preferably those like Verdana that work well on screens.
- Consider help for the visually impaired or sound options for the hearing impaired.
- Look at other sites you like and borrow the best ideas.
- Keep copy short and punchy.
- Keep your content regularly updated.

Create sensible links and navigation so that visitors can search and use your site in a natural and logical fashion. Use a child to test it – they'll soon tell you what sucks and what's cool.

Making money

- You can only make money from your site if visitors can find it so you can't just publish it on the internet and hope that, magically, visitors will find it and turn you into a millionaire. Out of sight – out of mind! Repeat purchasing is often a function of 'recency and frequency' too. If visitors only buy your product once a year (e.g. car insurance) – what else can you get them to come back for?

- **Search engines** work in a variety of different ways but mostly they use things called spiders and robots to look for words or phrases that match the search strings the customer has put into the search engine they use. So if I type in an exact web address it will find it easily enough. If I'm looking for bed and breakfasts in the Peak District it could throw up a whole range of options and yours may or may not be one of them. You can pay relatively cheaply through the **Google adwords** programme to get your site higher up the search listings and also have ads from which you can create revenue piped onto your site. It's called 'pay per click' advertising.

- You can also find other complementary sites and ask to **swap links** with them, because the more sites yours is linked with the more the search engines will pick up your address.

- You can join or use **affiliate marketing programmes** like Trade Doubler, Commission Junction and Affiliate Futures where you advertise other companies' products on your site and you receive a small commission if the visitors click through from your site to theirs and buy something.

- The big issue, however, is getting regular recognition for your site from other sources, so:

- o You need to put your web address on your business cards, your company stationery, brochures, mugs and mouse mats, anything printed basically.
- o Get regular mentions on the radio, the local or national press, TV if at all possible.
- o Send out a press release at least once a month to keep interest going.
- o Ensure you use devices like newsletters, and 'tell a friend' (viral marketing) to keep visitors coming back to your site – it's called 'stickiness'.
- o Speak at your local Chamber of Commerce, trade events, etc.
- o Give away free stuff like documents and guides on your site.
- o Be creative, constantly, or your visitors will forget you are there.
- Consult and use your web traffic statistics packages regularly so that you can see where your visitors go and what they are interested in. If something isn't working, experiment, change it until it does work or drop it.

Security

- People really worry about hackers and identity theft for good reason so make sure that you can assure your visitors that their payment transactions are safe using something like Verisign, WorldPay or PayPal.
- If you ask your visitors to share personal details make sure you are registered under the Data Protection Act.
- If you use tracking devices like cookies you must tell your visitors.
- You must take all reasonable steps to protect your systems from hackers or other system failure – choose your web host carefully.

Chapter 13 Running your own retail business

Napoleon once said that the British were a nation of shopkeepers and so we are! Running a retail outlet is a very common new lifer ambition.

Retailing has always been big business in the UK, with sales in the sector worth over £265 billion in 2007 (larger than the combined economies of Denmark and Portugal). Naturally the sector is highly susceptible to economic and consumer trends as illustrated by the current climate.

- 1% of all enterprises in the UK are retailers, with 184,695 VAT-registered businesses operating in 278,630 retail outlets.
- Almost 8% of GDP (Gross Domestic Product) is generated by the retail sector.
- The retail industry employed over 3 million people as at March 2008, which equates to 11% or approximately one in nine of the workforce.

As with any business, all the information in Chapter 8 on planning and financials is still absolutely vital but there are a few additional issues in retail that make it a more unique challenge. The prevalence of the major chains has created some difficulties especially regarding price competition and of course some opportunities. Naturally, your first store could be so successful that before you know you'll have a presence on every high street, but first things first.

Find your niche

You need to see if there's an obvious and preferably unique gap in the current market for your retail idea. If there is, is that because you've thought of something nobody else has, or have others tried before and found that the gap is there because there's no business to be had? If you can't compete on price with the Tescos (Britain's top retailer) or the Top Shops of this world, what else will you bring to the party and how do you know that there are enough people around who will be willing to pay in sufficient numbers for what you have to offer? Good niches tend to be in specialist areas that the big boys won't touch (yet!) – antiquarian books, exclusive designer goods in fashion or for the home, rarities, anything offering depth of stock or specialist service expertise.

Choosing your site – bricks and mortar

Retail is all about location, location, location. Customers generally need to find you easily or to be drawn in as passing trade. The more prime a location is considered, the more expensive the lease or freehold will be. What works for one retailer, however, might not work for another. If you're focused on convenience then you'll want to be close to your target customers, perhaps have access to parking and so on. Selling specialist goods such as furniture may give you a wider catchment area for customers and as it is what's known as destination shopping, you can be located away from the high street. You may want to be located in a cluster with other lifestyle type shops – designer shoes, clothes, jewellery, etc.

Rents are usually calculated on the basis of square footage, location and any additional features that might make it more attractive, e.g. period features, stockrooms, potential for expansion, etc. Getting involved with leases needs expert help so don't sign anything without legal advice. If a shop lease only has a couple of years to run you may need to be sure that the owner will offer you first refusal on a renewal, and an indication of what the new cost is likely to be, or you could spend money on fittings that would be wasted and build a business that could falter if it has to move somewhere less favourable. The cost of business rates also needs to be taken into account, as does access for delivery vehicles, refuse storage, etc.

For online retailing you should also check out Chapter 12 – the web entrepreneur.

Assess the competition

You should always study other similar businesses in your target area. The chances are that the competition will always be around. If you are aiming to complement what's already available, rather than going head to head with established businesses, you might avoid a price war. For example, if there are plenty of thriving businesses selling designer clothes but there is a dearth of shoe shops like the one you want to set up, your shop is generally more likely to have a higher chance of success. Find out what the size of the local population is and any other relevant demographics that would help you to work out if there is room for a business like yours or *another* business like yours. Go and be a customer of your competitors (or encourage friends and family to do it for you), study gaps and what works so that your business will have the edge. Be more specific and watch or count their footfall (the number of customers in and out), how many come out empty handed, how many come out fully loaded, what are the busy days and times. How much money do you think they're taking? In her book *Anyone Can Do It*, Sahar Hashemi of Coffee Republic fame writes a very interesting account of how she watched other coffee shops like this to work out their potential business before they opened their first shop. Simple but effective.

Decide what to sell and find suppliers

Make sure you think very carefully about the products you're going to stock and why. Who are your target market customers and what do they want to buy? The best retailers are good at providing well-edited collections of merchandise that customers can rely on. Most people set up specialist shops because it's a passion with them already or they have some previous work experience in the area. You need to plan ahead especially if you are selling seasonal goods because all the trade fairs and so on will be fixed in advance and you can't open in the autumn with last summer's stock. You can use internet searches and trade magazines to locate new merchandise before you start trading. Once you are trading, you may find that new suppliers will approach you.

One of my favourite local retailers offers an excellent case study in this regard. They started out as a family-owned sports store. Once the likes of JJB moved into town they realised that they had to re-invent themselves or they wouldn't survive, because they couldn't compete on price and the additional service they provided wouldn't be enough to protect them. They decided to get into the sports casual clothes market with Australian brands like Quicksilver and they've never looked back. They have recently expanded the interior of the store, stocking young teen brands and menswear downstairs with older teens and 'yummy mummy' appeal stock upstairs. Each area has its own identity – sporty and masculine in the men's area, boudoir style with lovely mirrors and antique cabinets housing jewellery upstairs. Now they stock range extensions such as costume jewellery, handbags and footwear. They've kept the expensive niche sportswear for skiing and designer sunglasses, but they've ditched the football shirts and gym knickers. Their prices range from a few pounds for a pair of designer earrings to a couple of hundred for a good coat or jacket and they have exclusive stockist agreements with top mid-market brands. They do very well, they have a loyal customer base and they deserve to. So could you.

Stock level management is critical – you must be sure that you can reorder products that sell well, but also that you don't get stuck with a stock room full of merchandise nobody wants. Suppliers are often wary of new start-ups and you may have to work hard to get the right credit terms on which to run your business. If a supplier already has a stockist in the area they may be reluctant to supply you however much you beg and plead. They will want to protect their exclusivity and relationships with long-standing buyers. Many will also have rules about mark ups – for example, apparel is usually 300% – and some may help with special stock for sales and point of sale materials like posters and so on. Stock turnover or sales per square foot are a critical performance indicator in retailing so make sure you know your numbers and monitor them carefully. I can usually tell if new retail businesses are going to last when I first walk in – if they don't have enough stock (and of the right kind) turning over quickly enough to cover the expenses of rent, rates, heating, lighting and staff then they will be out of business very quickly indeed. Retail can be a harsh mistress as well as a beguiling one.

Set up shop

Once you've decided on where you want to be and the type of premises you want, you will have to consider your layout, equipment and decor. You need to be sure that the atmosphere is right for what you're selling. Creating a great customer experience is what will make you successful so don't skimp on it. What about mood music? For clothing stores how good are the changing rooms, lights and mirrors? Have you provided a 'male crèche' with comfy chairs and magazines for shop weary partners or an activity area if your customers are likely to bring in their children? Don't forget the practicalities either: can people move around easily, especially if they have buggies or wheelchairs? Is there enough space for all your stock? Are there enough cash registers and sale points? Can you see blind points that might encourage shoplifters?

Using technology

Technology can help retailers in many ways. There are all sorts of options when it comes to tills, stock control, security tagging, bar coding and managing customers for marketing purposes. You could even set up an online shop as well as having your bricks and mortar presence. A friend of mine in Norfolk who runs a cool menswear store is doing a roaring trade from his web business in designer sports glasses now, which he set up quite opportunistically after a couple of enquiries from customers in London found he was a dealer in their favourite brand and stocked the styles they couldn't buy locally.

What does your brand and customer experience stand for?

Having a strong and consistent brand identity is highly beneficial to your company. What do you want your brand to be synonymous with? Quality? Convenience? Reliability? Choice? Price? Will you be 'never knowingly undersold' like John Lewis? Brands are more than just logos over the door or on your carrier bags; they must have real substance. Do your staff, for example, live up to your brand or are they haughty, rude, uninformed, unhelpful and scare customers away? Everything you do reinforces the image you want to project.

Marketing and promotion

Right from the beginning you'll want to make your opening day a success with some pre-launch publicity so that customers know you are there. Local newspapers and radio stations are always keen to promote local businesses in their communities so that they can maximise on advertising revenues in the future and they are usually very pleased to welcome good content. If you offer an exclusive competition in conjunction with them, they'll be even keener to partner you because they love to get something for nothing and add value to *their* customers. You won't have opened your business unless you're proud of it so don't be shy and make as much noise as possible.

Once you've opened, though, you need to keep up the momentum. Inviting customers to become part of special member clubs where they get discount shopping nights, first pick of new stock, wine or food tastings, free gift wrapping at Christmas, fashion shows, etc., can all help you build the relationships with customers that will be vital to your success.

Check the law

You must make sure that you comply with all relevant legal requirements. Retail has many specific pieces of legislation that affect it such as the Sale of Goods Act, the Distance Selling Act, Sunday Trading Laws, Weights and Measures legislation, returns and refunds, warranties and complaints, consumer credit – and of course you should be familiar with the role of Trading Standards. There are also considerations that your local planning office might need to help you with regarding access for those with disabilities, staff and customers alike. You can find more detailed information on the Business Link website, under 'Selling and marketing'.

You may also need to take the appropriate insurance covering stock and the normal fire and theft issues and public liability insurance.

Hiring staff

It's likely that you'll be employing some members of staff even if you intend to work in your business yourself most of the time. You will probably need part-timers or Saturday staff to help you at busier times or while you are doing other things such as: buying, stocktaking or just having a rest stop. Make sure you're familiar with all the red tape as usual and choose your staff carefully – they are your brand as far as the customer is concerned. Always take up references, too, if you don't know them: shrinkage is a specific problem in the retail trade and not just because of customer shoplifters.

Financials

Every business has certain, shared key elements that have to work and be considered – cash flow, overhead recovery, etc. Retail has its own unique ones as I've already mentioned and you ignore them at your peril – sales per square foot, stock turnover (preferably sell it before you have to pay for it), pilferage (staff and customers), sales mark downs for clearance, margin protection. If your profits are always tied up in your stock and you can't or don't sell it then it can become a vicious cycle of cash flow struggles. I don't want to put you off but to make sure you go into business with your eyes wide open.

If you invest £100,000 in stock with a 300% margin, your maximum possible income on that stock is £300,000. The more regularly you can sell your stock investments the more money you can make. However, if you consider that you will need to allow for shrinkage, lower margins for sale stock, stock costs you never recover because they don't sell minus all your expenses, you can start to create a basic scenario of your sales forecasts, breakevens, cash flows, profit and loss, etc.

Essential resources

www.brc.org.uk British Retail Confederation

www.taforum.org The Trade Association Forum established in 1997. Housed along with the Confederation of British Industry (CBI). Website contains a search facility for all the different trade associations in the UK.

www.britishchambers.org.uk British Chambers of Commerce

www.businesslink.gov.uk Business Link

Chapter 14 Running your own hospitality business

Another popular new lifer dream is to give up a mainstream job and open a restaurant or a tea shop, run a pub or open a bed and breakfast (B&B), here or abroad.

Once again, if you have no prior work experience or connections in this area you will need to prepare yourself thoroughly beforehand so that your fondest dream does not become your worst nightmare. Like retail, these businesses can seem to be simple to run from the outside but real professionals always make success look effortless. The hospitality business usually means long and unsociable hours: you're busy working to help others have fun and relaxation. Again, I'm not trying to put you off because such businesses can be highly rewarding but ask Gordon Ramsay and he'll probably tell you that it's all about planning, imagination, passion and good old-fashioned hard work. It's easy enough to try out a part-time job in a business like this and get some experience so why not do that first before you take the plunge?

What I can never understand is why those who choose to run these businesses don't get the fundamentals right. I have had to travel a lot for work, I started my management career in the hospitality industry and I'm a bit of a food and travel junkie at the best of times so I have a pretty broad spectrum of experiences (and opinions you'll note!) in this area. The clue about what is important is usually in the title, though. If you're going to open and run a successful bed and breakfast establishment then you must as a starting point and bare minimum have comfortable beds and offer a decent breakfast. I recently had to stay in a B&B in Shropshire as a guest at a family wedding. It was quite expensive, being in a touristy area, but the mattress I had to sleep on was so bowed and buckled I could barely walk for a week afterwards. The breakfast was OK but thumbs down for the bed. I've stayed in hotels where the showers have barely spluttered out a cupful of hot water (no fun when you're already covered in soap suds and late for a meeting!). People live in much more comfortable homes than they used to so pre-war Britain standards, or Fawlty Towers-like establishments just don't wash any more. I've been served food so dreadful in restaurants I can scarcely believe that they employed a monkey in the kitchen let alone a chef. Hygiene is also an absolute, basic must. So here as a starting point, and in marketing-speak, are the core propositions of your establishment.

- Pubs must sell well-kept beer, in clean glasses.
- Tea rooms and coffee shops must provide fresh, hot, beverages in clean, unchipped cups, and have comfortable chairs.
- Restaurants must sell flavoursome, well-cooked food with clean crockery and cutlery.
- Hotels and B&Bs must provide clean comfortable beds; free flowing hot water and a good breakfast.

After that you can be as creative as you like because the ambience you develop for your target market and the customer experience you host becomes your all-important point of differentiation. If you take over an existing business, it is worth making sure that you can afford to replace their terrible beds and crockery before you start re-trading under new management or you will be as unsuccessful as the people who sold it to you!

So why do you think that your customers will want to come to your establishment? Will you provide what they want? Will they come more than once? If you are running a busy pub primarily for youngsters or singles who are interested in hooking up with someone, then lively music, contemporary furnishings, tapas to share and a condom machine in the toilets is probably spot on. If you want to attract sophisticated couples in a country setting then the same treatment won't work. You'll probably be able to make money from a gastro-pub menu and a decent wine list but with background noise/music that allows people to chat to each other or read the paper in peace.

The thing about the UK is this – our hospitality industry has a terrible reputation, although not always deservingly, but people don't complain here. They will simply not visit your establishment again and they will tell other people not to patronise you either. The power of word of mouth recommendation or condemnation is king in this marketplace more than any other.

Location is as important as it is for retail but will be entirely dependent upon your target market. Business hotels need to be near good transport networks; retreats need to sometimes give the illusion of being far way but still be accessible by road; tea rooms need to be accessible by foot and usually near good shopping locations.

There are two common methods of **finding premises**. You could either buy somewhere and custom build, i.e. turn an old watermill into a country hotel and restaurant, a shop space into a café (which will certainly involve you with an architect and the local planning authorities), or buy something that is an existing going concern. Websites such as Daltons Online **(www.daltons.co.uk)** can be a useful place to search, or just keep your eyes peeled in the areas you are interested in, and talk to local estate agents (some specialise in commercial properties). Either way you usually need quite deep pockets although these businesses usually offer accommodation, so many people sell their homes to finance their ventures.

The hospitality trade is subject to **legislation** that applies to all businesses, some shared with retail, such as Weights and Measures, as well as some unique ones particularly around food hygiene, the licensing act and so on. Under-age drinking and drug abuse, date rape drugs, etc., are all things that publicans and licensees must know about.

The marketing, staffing and technology pointers are pretty similar to the ones mentioned in retail. However, low-paid jobs in hospitality, like washing up, cleaning and so on, generally seem to involve migrant workers and are the lifeblood of the black economy so be extra careful that you are on the right side of the law when employing your staff. The internet is a perfect marketing tool for this trade so you can post special offers, prices, menus, directions and maps for customers to find you, photos of rooms, local attractions and so on. Check out services such as Top Table and the Tourist Board in the Essential resources.

Essential resources

www.guysimmonds.co.uk Training and information for those who want to run a pub, restaurant or hotel.

http://rrgconsulting.com Restaurant resource group. American site but offers some excellent free resources, ideas and templates.

www.fabjob.com/restaurantowner.asp Offers a free e-book on setting up your own restaurant.

www.caterer.com Prime recruitment resource for jobs in catering.

www.flva.co.uk Federation of Licensed Victuallers Associations. Looks after the licensed trade.

www.toptable.co.uk Marketing association for restaurateurs.

www.culture.gov.uk/tourism Essential site containing all the relevant trade association links.

Chapter 15 Re-training and self-development

'People cannot be expected to learn one expertise and just apply it routinely in a job. Your expertise is in steadily renewing your knowledge base and extending it to new areas. That lifelong cycle of learning really is the foundation of the new information organization and economy.' *George Gilder*

Being made redundant is often a time when people might wish that they'd spent more time developing themselves and getting recognised qualifications than they have. Being on the job market without certain skills (particularly basic literacy, numeracy and IT skills) can make getting an interview, let alone an offer, very tough indeed. Learning really is for life and you're never too old to pick up a few new tricks. Creating a record of Continuing Professional or Technical Development (CPD, CTD) for yourself and being able to demonstrate your commitment to it can make a big difference when it comes to getting a new job offer or holding on to the one you've already got. The Chartered Institute of Personnel and Development (CIPD) *Barometer of HR trends and prospects 2009* revealed that 33% of job leavers cited the lack of development or career opportunities as their reason for leaving. The all-party commons Public Accounts Committee reported in July 2005 that there were currently between **700,000 and one million over-50s** who wanted to work but were unable to find jobs. Many over-50s may continue to be discriminated against because they lack the skills needed by employers – who can quite legitimately rule them out when sifting through job applications and selecting candidates for interview. So if that's you, read on!

Creating a new life might also involve embarking on a **completely new career direction** or **setting up your own**

business. If you've worked for big corporate organisations all your life you may well find that that doesn't necessarily equip you to run a start-up venture. If you've been used to paying agencies to do your PR or marketing, having an assistant to do all your admin and an IT support desk to deal with your technology hiccups, you could have a rather rude awakening when you have to do this yourself. So, you may need some of the specialist training help I have mentioned in Chapters 8 to 14.

You will probably also want to research the Essential resources listings in this section and the training pages of www.newlifenetwork.co.uk to discover how to give your skills a spring clean or pick up some new ones. Adding to your skill set while you are working on getting your next job can be therapeutic as well as useful. You could also do some recreational study. Most Further Education colleges run classes as diverse as photography and website building. Better still, if you have a particular expertise that might translate well into a short course, offer to set one up and run one.

If you are in work, make sure you take advantage of whatever training opportunities your employer makes available to you. If you want to change jobs make sure your future employers have some kind of development programme you can take part in. Programmes such as 'Chartered Manager' through the Chartered Management Institute are increasing in popularity as a way of gaining acknowledgement of both study and achievement. The Institute of Leadership and Management also offer management qualifications at team leader and supervisory levels which can be run in-house or as day release options. You could lobby to get your company to investigate the many tailored and often subsidised educational offerings through the local Business Link or Adult Education services. If you want some kind of benchmark to frame your training choices you could check out the National Occupational Standards for

Management and Leadership at **www.management-standards.org** that they hope will become a standard reference point for managers and education providers across the UK.

The standards cover six key categories:

1. Managing self
2. Providing direction
3. Facilitating change
4. Working with people
5. Using resources
6. Achieving results

Learning styles

Whether you have been used to formal learning programmes or not, finding out about your learning style can also be very important to choosing your study method.

You can go to sites like **www.vark.com** to complete an online survey to discover your learning preferences and strategies for improving your learning. It will help you to understand if you synthesise information best through, for example, visual or written means, by listening or by rolling up your sleeves and getting stuck in. If you prefer listening to information, you might want to buy or borrow some audio books. If you prefer to learn by doing, you could perhaps join practical workshops or volunteer your services for free so you can learn on the job. Most people can learn 'multi-modally', i.e. by using all the styles, but may prefer a particular sequence (e.g. read the instructions first, then look at a diagram, then try to practice the skill) or with a particular bias (e.g. more reading or more visual learning from films or videos). There are also SWOT (Study WithOut Tears) tips on the site for retaining information – especially useful if you need to take an exam and haven't any or recent experience of doing so.

Peter Honey and Alan Mumford (**www.campaign-for-learning.org.uk**) also identified another type of learning style preference. They maintained that if you identified your preferred style, you could apply it in a structured way to learning new things. Most of us use elements of more than one learning style, so you should think about your strongest and your weakest style to identify how you learn. If you're able to use your natural style, you're likely to find learning much easier and quicker. The four categories Honey and Mumford identified are:

- activists
- reflectors
- theorists; and
- pragmatists

Activists like to be involved in new experiences, tend to be open minded and enthusiastic about new ideas but get bored with the actual planning of implementation. They do, however, enjoy getting their sleeves rolled up and doing things. They can be impulsive, tending to act first and consider the consequences afterwards. Activists enjoy working in teams but do tend to hog the limelight.

Activists learn most when:

- involved in new experiences, problems and opportunities
- interacting with others in business games, team tasks, role-playing
- thrown in at the deep end with a difficult task

- chairing meetings, leading discussions

Activists learn least when:

- simply listening to lectures or long explanations
- reading, writing or thinking by themselves
- absorbing and understanding data
- precisely following detailed instructions

Reflectors prefer to stand back and look at a situation from varying perspectives. They like to collect a variety of information and views, and consider everything thoroughly before coming to any conclusions or making decisions. They enjoy observing others and will listen to their views before joining in and offering their own.

Reflectors learn most when:

- observing individuals or groups at work
- they have the opportunity to review what has happened and thing about what they have learned
- producing reports and analyses, performing tasks without tight deadlines

Reflectors learn least when:

- acting as leader or role-playing in front of others
- performing tasks with (in their view) no time to prepare
- being thrown in at the deep end
- being rushed or pressured by deadlines

Theorists like to adapt and integrate observations into complex and logically sound theories, thinking problems through with a precise step-by-step methodology. They can be perfectionists who like to fit things into a rational scheme, being objective and analytical rather than subjective or emotive in their thought processes.

Theorists learn most when:

- they are put in complex situations where they have to use their skills and knowledge
- in structured situations with a clear purpose
- offered interesting ideas or concepts even though they are not immediately relevant
- they have the opportunity to question and probe ideas behind things

Theorists learn least when:

- they have to participate in situations that emphasise emotion and feelings
- an activity is unstructured or the briefing is poorly executed
- they have to carry out tasks without knowing the principles or concepts involved
- they feel they're not on the same wave-length as other group members e.g. with people of very different learning styles

Pragmatists are keen to try things out. They want concepts that can be applied to their job. They tend to be impatient with lengthy, abstract discussions and are practical and down to earth.

Pragmatists learn most when:

- there is an obvious link between the topic and job
- they have the opportunity to try out techniques with feedback such as role-playing
- they are shown techniques with obvious advantages, e.g. saving time or money
- they are shown a model they can copy, e.g. a film or a respected leader

Pragmatists learn least when:

- there is no obvious or immediate benefit that they can recognise
- there is no practice or guidelines on how to do it
- there is no apparent pay back to the learning, e.g. shorter meetings
- the event or learning is 'all theory' with no apparent application

Many people wonder why they weren't taught how to learn properly when they were at school. Do you recognise yourself and your behaviour, likes and dislikes in any of those examples? Understanding your preferences in this way can make a world of difference to your ability to learn and your enjoyment of discovering new skills and information. I have run a number of management development programmes where participants have exceeded both their own and their employers expectations of their performance quite significantly by harnessing the power of these insights into their own learning. You could also consider other techniques such as speed reading or learning how to create Mind Maps, as popularised by Tony Buzan. Most public libraries can give you access to a range of different study media and so can Adult Education centres. When was the last time you visited and supported your local library? Hurry up because a lot of them are being forced into closure and that would be a terrible pity.

Funding

Certain types of learning, especially core skills, are targeted for government funding so it pays to check out the latest arrangements with your local Adult Education provider. Some options such as Learn Direct and the Open University allow you to pay as you go to build up learning credits and there are various grants and cheap loans available, so check them out on a case by case basis. Some employers will even pay for certain types of courses as part of redundancy severance packages.

Essential resources

www.hotcourses.com The leading site to find any course in the UK; has the UK's largest and most accurate database of educational opportunities.

www.learndirect.co.uk A variety of courses; learn at your own pace online in easy modules.

www.businesslink.gov.uk Business Link – each region has a slightly different offering but they do make available subsidised and relatively inexpensive training programmes on a variety of business topics.

www.wiseowlslearn.org Learning advice for mature workers.

www.nec.ac.uk National Extension College

www.mba-courses.com Compare and research MBA costs and programmes worldwide.

www.open.ac.uk The Open University. For most courses there are no previous qualifications required to study; you have to be 18 when your course starts but there is no upper age limit. The Open University itself is ranked among the top UK universities for the quality of its teaching. Most courses last for six or nine months, and start from as little as £80 for Level 1 Study Skills modules to several thousands of pounds for graduate and Masters degrees.

www.managers.org Chartered Institute of Management – details of training and Chartered Manager Scheme.

www.lsc.gov.uk Learning and Skills Council, responsible for funding and planning education for the over-16s in England.

www.directgov.uk/adultlearning Course and financial support information.

www.management-standards.org National Occupational Standards for management and leadership.

www.vark-learn.com Free site to find out your preferred learning style.

Good reads

The Manager's Good Study Guide, Sheila Tyler, The Open University ISBN 0-7492-6766-6

Mind Laundry, Gerry Kushel, Thorogood Publishing ISBN 1-854182-34-X

Use Your Memory, Tony Buzan, BBC Books ISBN 0-563-20814-7

Use Your Head, Tony Buzan, BBC Books ISBN 0-563-20811-2

Chapter 16 Working overseas

When both the economic outlook and the weather are grey and gloomy it can be very tempting to think about a complete change of scene. New job? New country? New life? Well, why not? You might want to go permanently, just for a couple of years or have a grown up gap year working as a volunteer. Some organisations are using international mobility strategies as a positive way of retaining their top talent in times of downturn, others give people little say in the matter - the 'Shanghai, Mumbai or Goodbye' strategy as it's known in the trade. There are some great internet resources out there for you to do your homework; many are very student oriented but the ones listed at the end of the section are my top tips.

All the advice in the previous chapters still applies here. If you don't like the job you do (or used to do) in the UK, doing the same thing somewhere sunnier may not bring the changes you were looking for. You'll still be miserable but with a tan! Here are my other key pointers as food for thought.

- Don't underestimate the impact on your family, if you have one. Families need to make choices that are as life changing as emigration together or they don't get off to a great start.
- Will friends and extended family be able to visit easily? At all? Too easily?
- If you've never been to a country before, you do need to visit it first before you decide to move there permanently or for a reasonable length of time. It may be better than you imagined – or not as great.
- If you have children, will you be able to maintain their education in the way you would like? If you move with a big company they will often pay for school fees in the UK or at local expatriate schools.

- If the country you move to doesn't have English as its main language, how are your language skills? Working abroad, or the 'immersion technique', is a great way to improve language skills but you may need to have the basics in place first.
- What about pay and conditions? Do you understand the local rules on tax, pensions and the like? Will your sponsor company assign you an advisor to help you take care of your financial affairs?
- Will it be better to let your property here in the UK, if you have one, so you can stay on the UK property ladder and rent abroad?
- Will your qualifications be valid in the country you want to work in? There are sometimes difficulties with professional qualifications abroad in medicine, law, teaching and accounting, for example, as standards, rules and regulations can vary considerably.
- A move abroad may give you access to new avenues of employment you wouldn't be able to consider here. Courses in diving and sports instruction can be taken in the UK beforehand, as can TEFL (Teaching English as a Foreign Language) courses.
- Emigration usually operates on a points system. You need to understand what your points score might be and what key skills the countries you are interested in are trying to attract.

Essential resources

www.transitionsabroad.com Fantastic portal that has breadth and depth of information and options.

www.offshore.hsbc.com Most of the international banks have good resources in this area but this HSBC one is excellent.

www.outboundpublishing.com Emigrate 2009 is the top UK show for researching your options.

www.fourcorners.net Top UK resource for helping people to emigrate to Australia, New Zealand, Canada and South Africa.

Chapter 17 Working in the not-for-profit sector

According to the organisation **Working for a Charity** there are about 169,000 general charities within the UK employing 608,000 paid workers (231,000 part-time) and a further 13.2 million unpaid volunteers (942,000 full-time equivalent). In addition, there are an estimated 750,000 trustees who take responsibility (unpaid) for the governance of individual charities. The scope is therefore enormous and the sector is a significant employer within the UK economy. With new organisations and initiatives a constant feature of the sector, the need for new people, talent and skills is set to continue. Plus, there are plenty of opportunities for those who want to work overseas.

This is potentially a great area for new lifers to consider especially since 2005 was Year of the Volunteer and this has raised the profile of the sector quite considerably.

The fact that much voluntary work is unpaid or low paid doesn't mean, however, that they'll be falling over themselves to take you on. You need the right skills, the right attitude and the right values as well as the ability to be clear about what you can offer. Competition will be fierce for jobs in the better known charities and for those paying reasonable salaries so you must be prepared to make a good case for why you are the right candidate. Charities don't just need people who have altruistic values or an aspiration to do something worthwhile so be realistic with yourself first. They also operate in a very broad sphere – medical skills are always useful overseas but then so are agricultural or forestry skills, HGV driving and teaching, as well as other skills more associated with private sector businesses such as accounting.

- What are your transferable skills? IT, finance, direct marketing, medical, technical?
- Do they match what the sector needs?
- Could you learn the skills you don't have with reasonable speed? How flexible are you prepared to be?
- What experience might you already have in their sector (paid or unpaid)?
- Does your CV identify the right skills and experience?

When you start searching:

- Think very carefully about the type of organisation you will be joining and whether you are temperamentally/culturally suited to it, not just whether you have the right skills.
- Make sure you are wholly in sympathy with the aims, objectives and values of the charity you hope to work for.
- Meet as many people as you can who already work in the voluntary sector and ask their advice.

Finding work

Press

National press All carry ads but The *Guardian* probably carries more than most.
Local press The *Evening Standard* (Monday – London jobs supplement, Wednesday – Public and Community) for London-based charities; the *Metro* (Wednesday – Public and Community). Check your local and regional press for jobs in

local charities and in national charities with regional offices or with head offices outside London.

Charity press Third Sector (Haymarket Group), *VS Magazine* (NCVO), *Professional Fundraising* (Brainstorm Publishing).

Specialist press Specific charities' magazines; newsletters and notice boards. Some jobs are only advertised internally and unless you have access you won't hear about them – this is one of the many advantages of volunteering or knowing people on the inside.

Websites

Many organisations now use their own websites for advertising vacancies and there are an increasing number of recruitment websites which advertise voluntary sector jobs. See the weblinks on the New Life Network site **www.newlifenetwork.co.uk**.

Charity recruitment agencies

You may want to **call them first** to check which particular areas or levels of experience they require – and whether your skills mix is of interest – to avoid wasting time and resources. Often they recruit for a charity by placing an advertisement as well as trawling their own database. In addition to those listed below, some individual consultants offer recruitment advice to their clients and some of the major recruitment consultancies operating in the commercial sector will also occasionally have briefs from charities – usually the big ones.

Charity Action Recruitment 5-13 Trinity Street London SE1 1DB 020 7378 5441/ 5442

CF Appointments Lloyds Court, 1 Goodman's Yard, London E1 8AT 020 7953 1190

Charity Connections 15 Theed Street, Waterloo, London SE1 8ST 020 7202 9000

Charity People 38 Bedford Place, London, WC1B 5JH, 020 7636 3900

CR Search and Selection 40 Rosebery Av., London EC1R 4RX, 020 7833 0770

Eden Brown 222 Bishopsgate, London EC2M 4QD, 020 7422 7300

Execucare 34 Ebury Street, London SW1W 0LU, 020 7761 0700

Harris Hill Ltd 37 Market Place, Kingston upon Thames, Surrey KT1 1JQ, 020 8974 9990

Kage Partnership Linton House, 164-180 Union Street, London, SE1 OLH, 020 7928 3434

Oxford Human Resource Consultants 69 Observatory Street, Oxford OX2 6EP, 01865 510980

ProspectUs 20-22 Stukeley Street, London WC2B 5LR, 020 7691 1925

The Principle Partnership 156 Tooley Street, London, SE1 2TZ, 020 7940 4150

The direct approach

You can also select a few of your favourite charities and write to them or email them directly. Always send a covering letter with your CV in which you outline clearly what your skills are (don't forget to include word processing and any other IT skills) and the type of work that you feel you can do for them.

As usual, it's best to find out the name of the person to write to (just call the switchboard and ask) rather than using a generic 'Dear Sir/Madam' and always enclose a stamped self-addressed envelope as it ensures a speedier reply and that you are sensitive to the limited resources of your chosen charity!

Useful organisations

Charities Aid Foundation (CAF) King's Hill, West Malling, Kent ME19 4TA, Tel: 01732 520 000. Provides services to help donors make the most of their giving and charities make the most of their resources – in the UK and overseas. CAF publishes an extensive range of reports and directories on the voluntary sector and runs the annual charities conference each autumn.

Charity Commission Harmsworth House, 13-15 Bouverie St, London, EC4Y 8DP Tel: 0870 333 0123. Central regulatory body for charities in England and Wales.

Directory of Social Change 24 Stephenson Way, London NW1 2DP, Tel: 020 7209 5151. Publishing and training organisation for the voluntary sector – it also has a library, a bookshop and runs the annual three-day Charityfair event each spring.

Institute of Fundraising Market Towers 5th floor, 1 Nine Elms Lane, London SW8 5NQ, Tel: 020 7627 3436. Membership organisation offering training, information and advice to fundraising professionals and those wanting to become fundraisers.

National Council for Voluntary Organisations (NCVO) Regent's Wharf, 8 All Saints Street, London N1 9RL; Tel: 020 7713 6161. A membership organisation that provides information, publications, training and conferences as well as legal, financial, IT and fundraising advice.

Scottish Council for Voluntary Organisations (SCVO) Mansfield Traquair Centre, 15 Mansfield Place, Edinburgh EH5 6BB; Tel: 0131 556 3882

Wales Council for Voluntary Action Baltic House, Mount Stuart Square, Cardiff Bay CF10 5FH; Tel: 02920 431 700

REACH 89 Albert Embankment, London SE1 7TP, Tel: 020 7582 6543. Finds part-time voluntary work for business and professional people that uses their skills and experience.

Community Service Volunteers (CSV) 237 Pentonville Road, London N1 9NJ, Tel: 020 7278 6601. CSV have four types of volunteering opportunities:

- **Young volunteers** (16–35) who are placed in projects all over the country, living away from home, e.g. helping elderly people/children and adults with disabilities/homeless people. Tel: 0800 374 991.
- **Retired and senior volunteers** (50+) who work on projects in education, the environment and community care in the local community.
- **Student tutors** who volunteer in local schools for a morning/afternoon a week.
- **Employee volunteers** who are encouraged to volunteer in their community with the support of their employer.

You could also check out some of the following excellent specialist job sites and sources of information about the sector but don't forget to look in your local Yellow Pages or just use your networks of friends and contacts.

www.wfac.org.uk Working For A Charity exists to promote the voluntary sector as a positive career option for those seeking paid employment and to promote the opportunities and benefits of becoming a volunteer to people who wish to do unpaid work. Their website is fantastic and contains pretty much all you need to know in order to evaluate what you have to offer and where to look. I recommend that you check it out before you do anything else.

www.yearofthevolunteer.org A site to support the 2005 Year of the Volunteer campaign.

www.nationaltrust.org.uk Find hundreds of ways of volunteering your time with the National Trust.

www.gvi.co.uk Volunteer organisation for projects abroad.

www.volresource.org.uk All about working in the voluntary sector: job listings, specialist agencies and websites.

http://society.guardian.co.uk/voluntary/ Job site for charities and the not-for-profit sector.

www.jobsincharities.co.uk Information about the sector and job site for charities and the not-for-profit sector.

www.CharityCareers.co.uk, Job site for charities and the not-for-profit sector.

www.samaritans.org Tel: 08705 627282 The Samaritans, founded in 1953. Always in need of volunteers.

www.princes-trust.co.uk The Prince of Wales's charity to help young entrepreneurs and workers.

Chapter 18 Coaching

Coaching is becoming increasingly popular as a career choice as well as an option for people who need help developing their careers or their future in a more general context. Some may be making a living, some may be struggling. Like all the services offering one-to-one support, there is a limit to what price the market can bear (often depending on whether you are reaching clients through businesses or privately), how much activity you can realistically keep up and how much competition you face for clients.

Why coaching?

According to the industry gurus, individuals who engage in a coaching relationship can expect to experience fresh perspectives on personal challenges and opportunities, enhanced thinking and decision-making skills, enhanced interpersonal effectiveness, and increased confidence in carrying out their chosen work or life paths. Appreciable results in achieving personally relevant goals, productivity and satisfaction both at work and at home are also consistent with a commitment to improving personal effectiveness. Successful people can become even more successful with expert coaching, so it's not reserved for those who feel that they are starting from scratch.

It sounds great doesn't it? So, what's the catch?

Well, there are *countless* books on coaching, training organisations who offer to turn people into coaches and coaching companies/individuals who specialise in one-to-one client work. Coaching is a self-regulated industry and there are a lot of confusing claims and information when it comes to choosing a course or a coach. Prices vary, as well as methods and the track records and efficacy of the coaches and coaching organisations themselves. That said, like most things, done well coaching really can be a highly rewarding experience so I'll try to offer a little guidance – but *caveat emptor* (buyer beware) applies!

There are a number of questions that can be asked to assess the competencies of a coach and they can be useful whichever side of the fence you're on. For example:

• What are the coach's qualifications and what kind of experience and professional background does the coach have?

• What form of redress do I have if I'm dissatisfied with the coach?

• Does the coach subscribe to a professional code of conduct?

• Does the coach adopt a goal-setting approach to coaching?

Coaching can sometimes get muddled up with other forms of support or guidance (and the first four are usually offered by people who have had years of professional training) so to help you to understand the difference between coaching and other forms of support here is a list of key definitions.

Teaching* - the transfer of knowledge, which is often dictated by a curriculum as opposed to individual need. These days most in the teaching profession will tell you that it's all about facilitating learning for the student, not an endless round of 'talk and chalk'.

Therapy* - dealing with an individual's problems from the past to improve their future. Coaching is not therapy. Therapy often addresses dysfunction, whereas coaching enables a functional person to move forward and achieve greater success.

Counselling* - professional guidance on social, psychological, or personal problems.

* Teaching, therapy and counselling have state recognised qualifications, some requiring a medical background. Most require several years of practitioner study.

Consulting - the transfer and deployment of professional knowledge, expertise or experience.

Mentoring - pairing with an experienced and trusted advisor to provide advice on development and networking opportunities. Coaching does not primarily involve giving advice; it raises people's awareness of their own capabilities and is based on the assumption that people are naturally creative, resourceful and capable of achieving better results.

Coaching is concerned with establishing with an individual client what their reality is today and then clearly defining what their individual aims or intentions for the future are. Coaching isn't about providing a cosy opportunity to chat about problems and issues. It involves a focused discussion, in which goals are developed, clarified and prioritised so that clients can take the necessary steps to increase their performance and achieve their objectives. A coach works with the individual to produce a plan of action that they can follow with confidence. Coaching is impartial, neutral and non-judgmental. It is essentially helping people to help themselves; the individual is free to use their own will and create their own set of standards to be achieved in their own time. There are several different varieties of coaching, including life coaching, business coaching and executive coaching, and most coaches specialise in different aspects of these.

The International Coaching Federation defines coaching as: 'an ongoing partnership that helps clients produce fulfilling results in their personal and professional lives. Through the process of coaching, clients deepen their learning, improve their performance and enhance their quality of life.'

Becoming a coach

Coaches can come from many different walks of life. High-level coaches are often former executives; there are official and unofficial coaches in the workplace; some business schools offer forms of coaching; there are 'gurus' like Jack Black of MindStore and Anthony Robbins; and numerous individuals or freelancers working as associates by themselves or through dedicated coaching firms. The prices they charge vary enormously from £30 to £250 per hour, or in the range of £150 per participant per day for seminars.

When it comes to finding business (or being on the receiving end of coaching), HR departments may need coaches who can be useful in a variety of situations: assimilation coaching (for those new to a job), performance coaching (becoming better at certain aspects of a job), career coaching, coaching during projects, coaching during mergers and acquisitions, coaching to non-executive directors and coaching during outplacement.

So, if you really want to follow the career path into coaching, and you are sure that you have the right skills (listening and facilitation being two of them) and motivations, when choosing a course you may want to consider the following differentiators: what are the entry criteria? How is the programme structured? How much supervised practice does the programme include? Does successful completion lead to a recognised qualification? How many people will be on each programme? What is the ratio of trainers to students? Who are its alumni and faculty? Does it represent value for money?

Essential resources

www.associationforcoaching.com An independent non-profit organisation with the goal to promote best practice, raise awareness and standards across the coaching industry.

www.coachfederation.org.uk **The International Coach Federation** (ICF) is the largest worldwide resource for business and personal coaches, and the source for those who are seeking a coach. The ICF is a nonprofit, individual membership organization formed by professionals worldwide who practice business and personal coaching.

www.nlpworldwide.com training organisation

http://www.coachinc.com training organisation

http://www.coachingnetwork.org.uk/ResourceCentre/Training AndAccreditation/

Good reads

Executive Coaching: How to Choose, Use and Maximize Value for Yourself and Your Team, Stuart McAdam, Thorogood Publishing ISBN 1-854182-54-4

The Big Book of Me Nina Grunfeld, Short Books ISBN 1-904977-499-9

Website content index

The New Life Network website,www.newlifenetwork.co.uk is designed to complement this book providing additional access to free downloads of reports and templates, news stories and editorial, and many more useful website recommendations. Please feel free to visit the site as often as you like and don't forget to tell your friends and colleagues about it if you think they would find it useful. You can also keep up to date with what's new by signing up to our free newsletter online.

The website is very rich in content and we're constantly adding to it and changing it.

There are six basic sections

1. **Find recruitment and career events** – a diary of all major UK recruitment fairs, emigration events, franchise exhibitions, business start-up and work-life balance events throughout the year. Event managers can list their events here free of charge
2. **Career Diary** - topical news stories, comment, book reviews and editorial features. Previous articles can be retrieved from the career diary archive.
3. **Find a brilliant new job** – from choosing a new career direction to job hunting advice there are helpful website reviews, free spreadsheets for managing job searches and tracking website passwords as well as comprehensive listing of the top job boards, recruiter sites and Executive search firms. These are organised by specialism such as interim management, HR, IT, Finance etc. Each website carries a review so that candidates can decide if the site is worth a visit or not.

4. **Be your own boss** - practical tips and advice on start-ups and franchising, recommended books, home office setup tips, free document downloads and website reviews and links for further research on raising business capital and accessing support services.

5. **Training and education guide** – a comprehensive listing of UK training provider resources and websites covering everything from how to become a Doctor to a plumber.

6. **Redundancy help** - download free spreadsheets for getting your finances under control, find website links with reviews for further research and information such as the official BERR (Department for Business Enterprise and Regulatory Reform) redundancy web pages and how to claim unemployment and other benefits.

Summary of references and inspirations

You can find a constantly updated source of the best websites for job hunting, training etc. at www.newlifenetwork.co.uk.

Websites

www.startinbusiness.co.uk Information-rich site on everything you need to research before making a decision to buy an existing business, a franchise, becoming an agent or re-seller or starting from scratch.

www.businesslink.gov.uk Government site for business.

www.startups.co.uk Solid information site for start-ups.

www.smallbusiness.co.uk Help and tips especially for small businesses.

www.daltonsbusiness.com Lively site for looking at businesses for sale.

www.british-franchise.org This should be your first stop when researching franchising. Independent, in that it carries no franchising ads, but sponsored by all the UK retail

www.hotcourses.com Leading site to find any course in the UK. Has the UK's largest and most accurate database of educational opportunities.

www.mba-courses.com Compare and research MBA costs and programmes worldwide.

www.managers.org Chartered Institute of Management. Details of training and Chartered Manager Scheme.

www.directgov.uk/adultlearning Course and financial support information.

www.management-standards.org National Occupational Standards for Management and Leadership

www.vark-learn.com Free site to find out your preferred learning style.

www.statistics.gov.uk Office of National Statistics

www.berr.gov.uk Department of Business Enterprise & Regulatory Reform

www.transitionsabroad.com information portal that has breadth and depth of information and options.

www.wfac.org.uk Working for a Charity

Essential good reads

The Manager's Good Study Guide, Sheila Tyler, The Open University ISBN 0-7492-6766-6

Mind Laundry, Gerry Kushel, Thorogood Publishing ISBN 1-854182-34-X

Use Your Memory, Tony Buzan, BBC Books ISBN 0-563-20814-7

Use Your Head, Tony Buzan, BBC Books ISBN 0-563-20811-2

Executive Coaching, Stuart McAdam, Thorogood Publishing ISBN – 1-854182-54-4

The Big Book of Me Nina Grunfeld, Short Books ISBN 1-904977-499-9

Back to Work – A Guide for Women Returners, Diana Wolfin and Susan Foreman, Robson Books ISBN 1-86105-588-9

Great Answers to Tough Interview Questions, Martin John Yate, Kogan Page ISBN 0-7484-4356-1

Why you? CV messages to win jobs, John Lees, McGraw Hill ISBN 13-978-007711510-4

Stress at Work – Management and Prevention, Jeremy Stranks, Elsevier ISBN 0-7506-6542-4

Who Moved My Cheese?, Dr Spencer Johnson, Random House ISBN 0-0918-1697-1

The Rules of Work, Richard Templar, Prentice Hall Business ISBN 0-273-66271-6

What You'll Never Learn on the Internet, Mark H. McCormack, HarperCollins Business ISBN 0-00-653206-3

Power: The 48 Laws, Robert Greene and Joost Elffers, Profile Books Ltd ISBN 1-86197-488-4

Financial Times Management Handbook, 3rd Edition, Prentice Hall ISBN 0-273-67584-2

Think and Grow Rich, Napoleon Hill, Wilshire Book Company ISBN 0-87980-163-8

Anyone Can Do It: 57 Real-life Laws on Entrepreneurship, Sahar and Bobby Hashemi, Capstone ISBN 1-84112-204-1

Feel the Fear and Do It Anyway, Susan Jeffers, Arrow Books ISBN 0-09-974100-8

Acknowledgements

My particular thanks go to:

Andrew Taylor who inspired me to start this whole thing off and who has now written a book about his experiences 'Burn the Suit!', Capstone, ISBN 978-1-841-12776-7

Richard Franklin and the team at arima publishing without whom this book would never have got into print.

All those who write to me and offer help and resources via the website.

My family for putting up with my incessant typing, and my Doctor for sorting out my RSI problem!

Sally Simmons and Rosalind Horton at the Cambridge Editorial Partnership for doing a great editing job.

Breinigsville, PA USA
18 August 2009
222540BV00001B/79/P